Barrier-Free Travel

Barrier-Free Travel

A Nuts and Bolts Guide for Wheelers and Slow Walkers

Candy Harrington

To order additional copies of this book, contact:
Xlibris Corporation
1-888-7-XLIBRIS
www.Xlibris.com
Orders@Xlibris.com

Contents

TO CHARLES

Acknowledgments

A project like this doesn't happen in a vacuum, so indeed there are many people to thank. However, I really detest those long and flowing acknowledgment sections, so I'll keep it short and sweet. I'd like to offer special thanks to the following people.

To Tracey Campbell, for making me realize that this project needed to be done, and it needed to be done now.

To Connie George (JWB), for letting me know when I put my foot in my mouth, and more importantly, when (and sometimes how) to extricate it.

To the hundreds of *Emerging Horizons* readers who shared their experiences, hints and resources with me over the years. I've tried to incorporate them all in this book so they'll be useful to others.

And last but not least, to Charles, for his constant patience, encouragement and love; and for taking charge of the lion's share of our domestic chores while I was otherwise occupied. And for the graphic work and copy editing. And (most importantly) for those weekend runs to El Pollo Loco for sustenance to keep our creative juices flowing.

Forward

It's A Jungle Out There!

It really is a jungle out there, especially as far as barrier-free travel is concerned. Travel, by its very nature, involves venturing away from the safety of home and hearth, and moving out and exploring unfamiliar territory. When you throw access issues into the equation, that unfamiliar territory can seem even more foreboding. Although travel can be an incredibly liberating and exciting experience, the mere thought of it can terrify the uninitiated. Why? Well, basically it's a fear of the unknown. Once you venture away from the safety of your home turf, you loose a certain amount of control. You're thrown out into the cold cruel world, and are placed at the mercy of strangers.

But it doesn't have to be that way. The nature of travel will never change, but with the proper preparation, you can change your own personal experiences. That's the main purpose of the book, to give you the basic tools to enable you to prepare for your journey. I'm not talking about travel agent type tools here. I'm merely referring to the nuts and bolts of barrier-free travel. The things that every traveler needs to know.

As the editor of *Emerging Horizons* I get a lot of feedback from travelers. Some of it is good, and some of it is bad. It goes with the territory that a certain amount of unexpected events do happen when you are out on the road. I used to think that I had heard every conceivable travel mishap story. That was before a gentleman told me the story about a 747 backing over his wheelchair. I'm not quite so smug any more.

The bottom line is that a lot of travel mishaps can be avoided. Some can be avoided with proper planning and self education on access rules and regulations. Others can be mitigated by playing a healthy game of "what if" before leaving home. And then there are those that just can't be avoided at all. No matter how well prepared you are, sometimes mishaps occur on the road. Chalk it up to bad luck. But, on the other hand, you can also have a run of bad luck at home. This book isn't the ultimate solution for avoiding all problems in regards to barrier-free travel. It is just a starting point. Combined with updated information on the internet, self education and experience, this book will help you navigate through some treacherous waters.

One of the biggest roadblocks to barrier-free travel is misinformation. So what's wrong with a little misinformation? Well if you rely on it and accept it as the truth, you may be in for a surprise when you take off on your holiday and find out it's incorrect. Furthermore, misinformation may even discourage you from exploring a locale that is indeed very accessible. In most cases, no information at all is better than incorrect information. Here are some of my favorite examples of misinformation.

Barrier-free travel is only possible in the United States. False. Access doesn't end at the US borders. In fact, some places even have stricter accessibility standards. Take Australia for example. Their maximum ramp slope for assisted or power wheelchair access is 1:14, and for manual wheelchair access is 1:20. The US standard is the steeper 1:12 for all access ramps. So, don't automatically rule out a foreign destination just because you think it may not be accessible. Keep an open mind and do your research.

Only the expensive properties have accessible rooms. False. All new properties (constructed after 1-26-92 in the US) must be built accessible. So check out budget hotels built after 1992 for the most accessible rooms.

The ADA covers air travel. False. Air travel is covered under the Air Carriers Access Act (ACAA) in the US. Learn your rights under this legislation.

Airlines are liable for all damage done to assistive devices (wheelchairs). False. Under the ACAA (covering US airlines) the liability limit for assistive devices is limited to the original purchase price (not the replacement cost) of the assistive device. Airline liability is limited to $9.07/lb. for international flights (under the Warsaw Convention). Make sure you have additional coverage if the value of your assistive device exceeds these limits.

So, as you can see, misinformation doesn't exactly help travelers. One of the goals of this book is to minimize the effects of misinformation. After all, if you know the truth, then a little misinformation can't really harm you. Armed with the correct information you can advocate for yourself, plan your own travel and you'll know what to do when things go wrong. And believe me, things will go wrong. Don't ever believe anybody who says you will have a trouble free trip. As I said earlier, sometimes mishaps will happen. The positive spin on that is that a little advance preparation helps you plan for the unexpected. This book stresses knowledge, and knowledge can help mitigate damages.

Like *Emerging Horizons* this book focuses primarily on travel for people with mobility disabilities. This book will educate you on access rules and laws and give you a good idea of what to expect once you hit the road. It will explain your rights as a travel consumer, and it will even tell you what to do when things go wrong. Like *Emerging Horizons* this book is about options and choices. It will give you resources and tell you where to look for answers. In fact, you'll find detailed contact information for all the resources mentioned in this book in the resource chapter.

There are of course also some things this book won't do. It won't patronize you or give you simplistic advice like "wear comfortable shoes." It also won't give you specific information about lodgings or sights or even give you a list of travel agents. It will however give you the resources to find out this information for yourself. I guess you could categorize this book as a "self help book about barrier-free travel." My assumption is that people want to take an active role in their holiday planning, whether they work with a travel agent or do it on their own.

And finally, if you know me personally, you also know that I'm a great proponent of the internet. So yes, there are some internet resources listed in this book. I make no apologies for that. In fact, the internet is the best place to find updated access information. Additionally, some internet based information is not even available in a non-electronic format. So, even if you personally don't have internet access, you might want to log on at your local library or ask a friend to help your surf the net. You'll be amazed at all the useful access information you'll find.

Of course, you may also wonder why I'm publishing this hard copy book if indeed I'm such a big internet fan. That's a fair question. Actually I've had the material and outline for this book for many years. The reason I didn't publish it was simple; I thought print material became outdated too easily. I still believe that to some extent, but thanks to some new technology I'm able to do something about it. The new technology will enable me to update this book on a more frequent basis. Access laws do change, and when they do, travelers need to know about them. So, it's my hope to keep this book updated to reflect such changes.

I've done my best to insure the accuracy of the information presented in this book; however regulations and laws do change. They are also subject to different interpretations. This book should be used only as a general guide, and should not be considered legal advice. If you want legal advice specific to your situation, consult a lawyer.

It really is a jungle out there; but that doesn't have to be a bad thing. In fact, a jungle can be a very pleasant place, if you have the right survival skills. And that's what this book will do; give you those survival skills. So read on and learn how to avoid the pitfalls, and then pack your bags, hit the road and enjoy that formerly forbidding jungle. And don't forget to send me a postcard!

Candy Harrington
PO Box 278
Ripon, CA 95366
horizons@EmergingHorizons.com

The contents of this publication are believed to be correct at the time of printing. Nevertheless, the author cannot be held responsible for any errors, omissions or changes in the information given in this guide, or for the consequences of any reliance of the information provided by the same.

1 | Up, Up, And Away

Air Travel

Everybody is flying these days. Indeed, air travel is one of the most popular forms of travel. Unfortunately, for people with disabilities, air travel can also be one of the most problematic areas of travel. Perhaps it's because there are just so many things that can go wrong on any given flight. And then again, perhaps it's due to the mountain of misinformation circulating around about accessible travel. I believe it's a combination of both factors; however, I tend to favor the misinformation theory, mostly because of my own experience with this growing phenomenon. So, what's wrong with a little misinformation? Well if you rely on it and accept it as the truth, you may be in for a rude awakening when you take off on your holiday and find out that it's incorrect.

Admittedly, it can be difficult to ferret out the wheat from the chaff, as far as misinformation is concerned. This situation is further complicated, by the fact that you can't always determine a person's credibility based on his or her position in the community. Just because somebody is a well respected professional, does not mean that they're also an expert on accessible travel. The story of Lenny the lawyer comes to mind here.

I had the great misfortune of meeting Lenny, a well-respected corporate lawyer, at a national disability conference a few years ago. I gave a presentation about accessible travel and Lenny was in charge of introducing me. He seemed harmless enough, until he opened his mouth. Lenny knew very little about accessible travel, but he obviously felt the need to include something of substance in his introduction. So he proceeded to tell the audience that Title II of the Americans with Disabilities Act (ADA) entitles all wheelchair-users to guaranteed bulkhead seating. Of course nothing could be further from the truth. He then informed the audience that he always manages to get bulkhead seats. He elaborated that he merely threatens to file a Title II lawsuit, and voila, the seats are his. Now I'm not arguing that Lenny could definitely be a major pain in the backside; in fact, if I were a reservation agent I would most likely give him the darned seats just to get him off the phone. But that's not the way things usually work in real life. And more important, Lenny the lawyer did my audience a real disservice by spreading this misinformation. Fortunately Lenny was not at all interested in hearing my presentation. He left immediately after the introduction; at which point I told the audience of the truth.

Although the Lenny incident is quite memorable, it's far from an isolated case. I've seen many other people spread misinformation; travel agents, rehabilitation professionals, and yes, even writers. Misinformation is rampant. So what's a traveler to do? Ask for documentation, and if somebody can't back up their claims with hard facts; then there's a good chance that they too are spreading misinformation. It's hard to argue with cold hard facts. With that in mind, let's talk about the facts of air travel.

Air Carriers Access Act—Contrary to the gospel according to Lenny, the Air Carriers Access Act (ACAA), covers air travel on all US based airlines. The ACAA outlines procedures which US airlines must follow, in regards to passengers with disabilities. Among other things, the ACAA mandates that people with a disability cannot be denied boarding, solely because of their disability. It also forbids airlines from assessing surcharges for the services mandated by the ACAA. Although many people take these rights for granted; consider the alternative. Here are a few examples.

KLM, a Dutch based airline, refuses to board non-ambulatory passengers who are not accompanied by an able-bodied escort. The official KLM policy on non-ambulatory passengers is as follows. "The passenger must be accompanied by an escort. They must fly on a wide body aircraft, on a flight with a duration of over 3 hours; and medical approval must be given (in advance) by KLM's Medical Department in Amsterdam." Even wheelchair athletes and other non-ambulatory passengers who live independently, have been denied boarding by KLM.

Other non-US airlines have similar policies, as a former Thai Airways passenger illustrates. "I was seated on a Thai Airways flight from Bangkok to Sydney, when I was approached by several airline employees and asked to disembark because I was a paraplegic. I refused, and the next 15 minutes were about as publicly humiliating as it gets. They wanted to know how I could use the toilet if I could not walk. They said I would have to deplane, because I was a safety risk, and I was unable to go to the toilet. I explained to them that I had traveled extensively throughout Southeast Asia, on my own. I then showed them my return airline ticket which proved I had already traveled from New Zealand to Thailand unaccompanied. I guess they decided that I wasn't much of a safety risk after all, as a few minutes later the plane started to taxi down the runway (with me on board)."

And finally, Ryanair, the Ireland based self-touted "low fare airline" actually charges extra to carry some disabled passengers. These charges are not reflected in Ryanair's published fares, as passengers are required to pay them directly to third-party contractors who provide wheelchair assistance at some UK airports. Contractors at these airports charge a "lift-on" and "lift off" fee of £12.50 per occurrence. A direct round trip involves 2 "lift-ons" and 2 "lift-offs", resulting in extra charges of £50 (Approx. $80 US). According to Ryanair CEO Michael O'Leary,

Ryanair only requires people traveling without their own wheelchair to pay these fees directly to the contractors. Interestingly enough, British Midland and Aer Lingus use the same airport facilities and contractors as Ryanair; however, these airlines don't require their passengers to pay directly for wheelchair assistance. Apparently both airlines absorb the charges into their general operating costs, and distribute them equally to all passengers.

As you can see, the ACAA affords travelers at least a minimum level of protection; a protection that is not found on many foreign air carriers. Now, you may hear from time to time that the ACAA also applies to non-US airlines. In fact, the Aviation Investment and Reform Act of the 21st Century (AIR 21) which was signed into law on 4-5-00, promised to extend portions of the ACAA to include non-US air carriers. So, where are we now with this "promise"? That depends on who you ask. According to a DOT spokesperson, "For now foreign airlines have been put on notice that AIR 21 exists and they are strongly encouraged to comply with the spirit of the law." On the other hand, many travel professionals doubt the feasibility of enforcing this regulation. Says one East Coast travel agent who specializes in accessible travel, "How can you enforce something without any specific regulations? Even when the regulations are set, I think it will be very difficult for travelers to enforce a US law on foreign soil, especially if they don't speak the language." Time will tell how much protection AIR 21 will offer. For now, the best advice is to proceed with caution, and operate on the assumption that only US carriers are required to abide by the ACAA.

The ACAA is a pretty straightforward piece of legislation; that is, until you get to the gray area of codeshare flights. A codeshare is a marketing agreement between 2 airlines, where one airline operates flights under the code of the other airline. Although not specifically addressed in the ACAA, an interesting settlement transpired in 1998 regarding a codeshare flight. The settlement stemmed from the following incident.

A wheelchair-user traveled unaccompanied from Seattle to New York on a United Airlines flight. He then tried to transfer to United flight 3516 to Frankfurt, Germany. This particular flight was a codeshare operated by Lufthansa Airlines. Lufthansa refused to board him, stating that he was a safety risk as he could not assist in his own evacuation in case of an emergency. Seeing as he had just traveled cross-country by himself, and wheeled himself down the boarding jetway unassisted, the passenger contended he could indeed assist with his own emergency evacuation. Still he was refused boarding. Under the terms of the settlement, neither airline admitted any wrongdoing, but both agreed to cease and desist from future violations. United paid a fine of $3000 and Lufthansa paid a fine of $1000. The moral of the story is to be wary of codeshares, as this settlement dealt with only the 2 airlines in question.

Always err on the side of caution. At the risk of sounding ethnocentric, use a US based carrier whenever possible. That way you know you're protected under the ACAA. To be fair however, Canada also has similar legislation called the Canadian Transportation Act. Other than that, watch your step, especially in underdeveloped countries. I've heard more than one story from wheelers who were stranded in the Caribbean because a non-US carrier refused to board them. Their only recourse was to purchase a higher priced same-day return ticket on a US carrier; a very costly option. Don't let that happen to you.

Know your Rights—Before you plan your flight, you should learn your rights under the ACAA. Once you have an understanding of the regulations, you will also have a good idea of what to expect as far as access in the air is concerned. Education and consumer awareness are the essential first steps to getting the services you need.

To that end, a great resource is *New Horizons: Information for Air Travelers with a Disability*, a pocket-sized guide which explains your rights under the ACAA. Get you free copy by calling the Paralyzed Veterans of America at 888-860-7244. The guide is small enough to carry in your pocket or purse, and I highly recommend that you take it with you when you travel. Somehow people just tend to take you more seriously when you can actually point out the law in black and white. Plus, it's also a handy reference. Of course the ACAA has been amended a few times since it's creation, so I also recommend reading both the seating amendment and the wheelchair damage amendment. Both amendments were published in the Federal Register; the seating amendment on March 4, 1998 and the wheelchair damage amendment on Aug. 2, 1999. It wouldn't hurt to carry a copy of these documents with you either.

Know Your Aircraft—Do you know the difference between an EMB-120 and a 777-200? Well, you should learn if you plan to travel by air. I'm not implying that you should become an aeronautical engineer; however, it really does help to know some of the basic differences between different types of airplanes.

Under the ACAA, US airlines are required to provide prospective passengers with basic information about the accessibility of their facilities, services, and aircraft. Such information can include facts like the location of seats with movable aisle armrests, the locations and dimensions of storage facilities for mobility aids, and the availability of an onboard accessible lavatory. As you might expect, some airlines do a better job of providing this information that others. For example, Continental Airlines has an excellent website (*www.continental.com*) that includes seating diagrams for all their aircraft, the location of the seats with movable armrests and even the dimensions of the cargo bin doors on their commuter aircraft. However, you can also obtain most of this information by phone. Don't be shy about asking for it, and remember to ask for it before you book your flight.

In the previous question, the big difference between the 2 airplanes is their size. The EMB-120 has 30 seats and the 777-200 has 383 seats. This is important, because most of the ACAA regulations regarding aircraft accessibility and boarding are referenced by aircraft size. Here are some important numbers.

The following ACAA rules apply to planes ordered after April 5, 1990 or delivered after April 5, 1992. Planes with 30 or more seats must have moveable armrests on at least half of the aisle seats; and airline employees are required to know the locations of those seats. Wide-body jets (those with 2 aisles) must have an accessible lavatory, and planes with more than 60 seats and an accessible lavatory must have an onboard wheelchair. Planes with 60 or more seats, that do not have an accessible lavatory, must carry an onboard wheelchair upon passenger request (48 hours advance notice required). And finally, planes with more than 100 seats must have priority space to carry at least one folding wheelchair in the cabin.

As far as boarding assistance goes, that too depends on the size of the aircraft. The ACAA mandates level boarding whenever possible on all aircraft with 30 or more seats. If level boarding is not possible, the airline is allowed to use a boarding device such as a lift, ramp, or stair climber. In aircraft with fewer than 30 seats, level boarding is not required. Airline personnel may use other mechanical boarding devices, as long as the passenger's physical limitations don't preclude using such devices. Under no circumstances are airline personnel required to hand carry a passenger on any aircraft with fewer than 30 seats. Airlines are required to maintain all lift devices, but even in the event of a mechanical breakdown, airline personnel are still not required to hand carry passengers on any aircraft with fewer than 30 seats.

Additionally, there are also a few aircraft that are considered exempt from the boarding assistance requirements of the ACAA. These aircraft are the Fairchild Metro, the Jetstream 31, and Beech 1900 C and D models. Boarding assistance (lifts) are not required for these exempt aircraft. According to the DOT, using a lift could create a significant risk of damage to these aircraft. Disability rights advocates are currently fighting this exemption, however for now it's best to steer away form these exempt aircraft.

Boarding options can also vary, depending upon the size of the airport. Not all airports have jetways to enable level boarding. Additionally even airports that do have jetways may not have a level boarding option due to heavy traffic. This is a common occurrence at many large international airports. If all gates are being used, even a large plane will park out on the tarmac, and passengers will deplane via boarding stairs. The passengers will then be bussed to the terminal. It's always a good practice to ask what deplaning procedures are available at your destination airport, just so there won't be any surprises.

Can advance planning and aircraft research really make a difference when it comes to air travel? Well, the story of my friend Elaine comes to mind. Elaine is a rather heavy lady and she uses an equally heavy power wheelchair. Elaine booked a flight on a small (25 seat) aircraft. When she arrived at the airport check in counter, the clerk asked Elaine if she could walk up a flight of stairs. Elaine informed the clerk that of course she could not. The clerk in turn told Elaine that she would not be able to board the flight. Elaine inquired as to why, and the clerk hemmed and hawed, but finally came out and told Elaine that she was too heavy for the lift, and too large to fit in the aisle chair. An argument ensued. Security was called. Things got ugly. In the end, the airline won out and Elaine had to reschedule her trip on a larger aircraft. It was an unfortunate incident, but the airline was well within their rights under the ACAA. A 1996 amendment to the ACAA states that "on aircraft with less than 30 seats, if a passenger cannot get to a seat that he or she can use, (i.e.: they are not able to fit in the boarding chair used on narrow aisle commuter aircraft, or unable to walk through a narrow aisle to a seat) the air carrier is not required to provide boarding (lift) assistance, as it is futile." Today when Elaine makes flight arrangements, she asks the airline how they board non-ambulatory passengers; and if they reply, "by lift", she then asks the weight capacity of the lift. She also asks for the width of the aisles and the boarding chair on smaller commuter aircraft. She then determines if she will be able to use the aircraft in question. Sometimes it takes 2 or 3 phone calls but Elaine vows never to make the same mistake again. She now realizes that a little advance research can save a lot of heartache and embarrassment. Live and learn.

Boarding Procedures—Although Elaine's story illustrates some of the problems you may encounter boarding a smaller commuter aircraft with a non-level entry; generally speaking boarding a larger aircraft from a level entry jetway is a pretty straightforward procedure. Of course, as always there are a few potential trouble spots, so you need to know the standard boarding procedure in order to understand your rights under the ACAA.

The first hurdle you will likely encounter is at the check-in counter. If you arrive with your own wheelchair or scooter, the ticket agent may insist that you transfer to an airport wheelchair at this time. Here's where you need to be a little assertive and insist that you stay in your own wheelchair or scooter. It's your right under the ACAA, to stay in your own wheelchair or scooter all the way up to the door of the aircraft. I strongly suggest you take advantage of this right, for a variety of reasons. First off, it's best to keep your own equipment with you as long as possible, because in theory, the less time the airlines have it, the less time they have to damage it. Also, as you may know, airport wheelchairs are not exactly what you would call comfortable, and you never know how long you will be stuck in one. It's not uncommon for flights to be delayed or canceled. Finally, you will loose a lot of your freedom if you give up your equipment. All airport wheelchairs come with a "wheelchair pusher", even if you can push yourself or if you are traveling with somebody who can push you. Your freedom (or lack of it) depends on the wheelchair pusher, and where he or she is allowed to take you. So, by all means, stay in your own wheelchair or scooter as long as possible. Don't fall for the old "it's our procedure" line when the ticket agent tries to get you to transfer to an airport wheelchair. It very well may be their preferred procedure, but remember you do have the right to refuse, and you do have a choice.

By the time you make it to the gate, you would assume all of your information (like the fact that you are a wheelchair-user) would be entered correctly in the computer. But, that's not the way it works in real life. Don't be alarmed if the gate agent looks down at you with amazement and says something incredibly intelligent like, "Are you on this flight?" Don't let comments like that worry you. Things will be all sorted out by the time you board the aircraft. The thing you should remember to do at this point is to tell the gate agent that you would like to preboard the aircraft. This means that you board the aircraft before the rest of the passengers. Preboarding has a lot of advantages. It gives you time to get settled and change your seat if you find out your assigned seat doesn't have a moveable aisle armrest, it allows you first crack at the overhead storage compartments, and it gives you priority storage for your folding wheelchair in the onboard closet. The airlines can't force you to preboard, but it really is to your advantage to do so.

When it is time for you to preboard, you will be transferred from your own wheelchair to an aisle chair. The aisle chair is a high backed chair with a pair of wheels in the back. You will be transferred to the aisle chair, belted in, then tipped back and rolled down the aisle to your seat. Upon request, you will be assigned a seat with a moveable aisle armrest. This makes transfers a lot easier, as you just flip up the armrest and slide over. Airline personnel will help you transfer to your seat if needed, however it's always best to tell them exactly how you would like to be transferred. Never assume they know anything, as they deal with a wide variety of passengers.

Now, if you just need a wheelchair for distance, there are a few other things to consider. The airlines will supply you with an airport wheelchair (upon advance notice) at check in. As I said earlier, the airport wheelchair also comes with a mandatory wheelchair pusher. Now, under the ACAA, airlines are not suppose to segregate people with disabilities and put them in special boarding areas; however, this sometimes happens to people who use airport wheelchairs. The airline rationale behind this is, that they don't force people with disabilities to wait in special areas, but they do require all people who use airport wheelchairs to wait in a designated area. They say this is done to keep track of airport wheelchairs, and it is only done at certain airports. At other airports the wheelchair pusher may not be allowed to let you stop anywhere, including the restroom. So, although this is a great service for people who cannot walk long distances, do be aware of the limitations. Best advice is to take some snack food and water with you, as you may not be able to stop and get anything to eat and drink. Also, if you connect from another flight, use the restroom on the airplane before you land (if you are able). If you travel with your own wheelchair, always ask for it to be brought directly to you at the gate. That way you won't have to use an airport wheelchair to get to the baggage area, or to your connecting flight. Generally speaking airport wheelchairs are a good option for people who can't walk long distances, but they are a hindrance for people who travel with their own equipment.

Seating—Seating is another source of great confusion. Who is entitled to what type of a seat, and how do you actually get it? First off, let me debunk a popular myth. Wheelchair-users are not always guaranteed seating in bulkhead areas. Some airlines will seat you there, some will not; but, it is not a right given carte blanche to all wheelchair-users under the ACAA.

Seating is actually addressed in the 1998 amendment to the ACAA. In regards to bulkhead seating, this amendment requires carriers to designate an adequate number of bulkhead seats as priority seating for individuals with a disability. These seats are required to be available to people who travel with a service animal or to people who have a fused (immovable) leg. Carriers also assign bulkhead seats upon advance request to anybody with a disability who self identifies himself as a person who needs this particular seating accommodation; providing those seats are not already assigned to other passengers. So, if you are a wheelchair-user (and you don't have a fused leg), you will be given a bulkhead seat only if one is available at the time of your request. Sometimes experienced travel agents can get bulkhead seats for their clients, sometimes they can't. Steer clear from any travel agent who guarantees you they will get you a bulkhead seat. There are no guarantees in life. The best advice is to make your travel arrangements as early as possible. Additionally, some airlines give priority bulkhead seating to all passengers who have a disability. Call all the airlines in advance to find out their individual policies on this matter, and then do business with the ones that will give you the seating accommodation you need. Of course, since this is an ACAA provision, it only applies to US airlines. I've heard from a lot of people who have requested bulkhead seating on non-US carriers, only to be denied this accommodation. Some non-US carriers even ask for medical documentation, and then still deny the request. And of course, they are within their rights doing this, because they are not subject to the ACAA.

Moveable aisle armrests are another story though. The same 1998 ACAA amendment requires airlines to designate an adequate number of seats with moveable aisle armrests as priority seats for individuals with disabilities. These seats are required to be available to passengers who use an aisle chair to board the aircraft, and who cannot readily transfer over a fixed armrest. Because there are a higher percentage of these seats, they are usually easier to get. Still, sometimes there can be confusion during boarding, as some airlines don't readily know the locations of these seats. It's usually not much of a problem, as the cabin crew will reassign you to another seat that does have a moveable armrest, even if they have to try to flip up every armrest on the airplane to find it. Another point to keep in mind is that bulkhead seats usually do not have moveable aisle armrests. All seating accommodation requests must be made at least 24 hours in advance. If a requested accommodation is made less than 24 hours prior to the flight, the airline will do the best they can to accommodate the request, but they are not required to move any other passengers from their assigned seats. And of course, all these seating provisions only apply to airlines that provide advance seating assignments.

Another source of seating confusion (and frustration) are the highly prized exit row seats. The criteria for exit row seating is pretty well established. You must be able to operate the emergency door (which weighs 70 pounds), be able to understand and follow directions in English, be over 15 years old, and be able to assist crew members in an emergency. Most wheelchair-users, or anybody who requires a wheelchair assist, won't intentionally be seated in an emergency exit row. However, it does happen. When it does, the cabin crew, (who is ultimately in charge of the safety of all passengers), will simply reseat passengers who are inappropriately assigned to exit row seats. The bigger problem with exit row seats, is that some airlines insist that the center aisle of the bulkhead exit rows are also exit rows. I have known people who received their priority seating in bulkhead, only to be told by the cabin crew that they would not be able to sit there because it was an exit row. I find this reasoning somewhat absurd because the same airlines routinely seat families (with kids under 15) in this row. Still, some employees do have it in their mind that this is an exit row; so if you find yourself in this situation, ask to have the Complaints Resolution Officer (CRO) resolve the matter. It is the quickest solution to this unfortunate situation.

And finally, a word about upgrades. Years ago, when fewer people traveled, wheelchair-users were routinely upgraded to first class. However, today those upgrades are few and far between. Partly because more people are traveling, and partly because the airlines are now giving those upgrades to their highest echelon frequent flyers. I shudder whenever I read a travelogue that even mentions a wheeler's first class upgrade. It's a great perk when it happens, but stories like that tend to create false expectations. Don't count on getting an upgrade. If you absolutely need that extra room, then buy a business class or first class ticket. There is no provision in the ACAA (or anywhere) which requires carriers to upgrade people with disabilities to first class. Now by all means, go ahead and ask for an upgrade at the gate, but don't be disappointed if you don't get it. My friend John has perhaps the best (or at least the most creative) "upgrade technique" around. John "tries to look as large as possible". Sometimes it works, but most of the time John ends up in coach with the rest of us.

When Nature Calls—What do you do when nature calls at 30,000 feet? That's a question I hear over and over again, as it's a major concern for first-time flyers. There are actually many solutions to the "toilet problem", but they all take some sort of advance preparation. I also have to stress here, that since everybody is different, what works for one person may not necessarily work for the next. Sometimes it takes a bit of fine-tuning and adjustment to find a method that works best for you. With personal experience you will be able to do this, but for now let me just outline your options.

One option is to travel on an aircraft with an accessible restroom. All post 1992 wide body aircraft must have at least one accessible restroom. All planes with an accessible restroom must also carry an onboard wheelchair. Although this is the standard procedure it's always best to request an onboard wheelchair when you make your reservations. How do you know if the aircraft you will be flying on has an accessible restroom? Well, this is one of the things the reservation agent should be able to tell you when you make your reservation. Actually, they may have to transfer you to another department, but the information is required (under the ACAA) to be available upon request.

Now don't get too excited about these airborne accessible restrooms, as they are a far cry from what you find on the ground. They are big enough to roll into with the onboard wheelchair, and they do have grab bars, but that's about as far as they go. Basically you must be able to transfer from the onboard wheelchair to the toilet, and unless you are a very small person you must be able to do this without assistance. Quite frankly there is not enough room for 2 adults in the accessible restroom, however a small adult an a child may be able to squeeze in at the same time. My friend Carol has perhaps the most astute observation about the onboard accessible restrooms. Carol can walk a few steps, and she uses a scooter for distance. She sums it all up by saying, "Well, at least I never have to worry about falling down in the accessible restroom on an airplane. There just isn't enough room to fall down." Still, if you can use the onboard wheelchair, and transfer independently, it is a good option. The flight attendants will help you use the onboard wheelchair, but their assistance ends once you reach the restroom door.

"Accessible" lavatory on Airbus 319 (Air Canada).

Some travelers totally write-off the onboard restroom, and wear a catheter instead. This is usually easier for men than women as men can use an external "condom-type" catheter while women have to use an internal catheter. If you don't normally use a cath-

eter, the downside (for women) is that you have to arrange for
somebody to remove the catheter when you get to your destination. And of course if you are on a long flight, you also have to
figure out a discreet way to empty your leg bag. I consider this a
learned skill, as I have heard from many people who manage
this feat, under the cover of a blanket. Of course you should
practice this procedure before you leave home (with the blanket). Fortunately most long flights have several movies, so the
cabin is dark for a majority of the time, and darkness does work
in your favor. I've also been told to make absolutely sure that
your transfer container is a leakproof, and that it has a very secure lid. I have heard about some unfortunate accidents, where
the lid came off the container while it was safely stowed in a
duffel bag. This can be very embarrassing, and quite difficult to
explain to customs officials.

Of course some people prefer a more personalized solution
to the bathroom dilemma. By this I mean many people
experiment with diets, vitamins, and limiting their fluid intake.
And in fact, many people swear by their personal pre-flight
regime; however I hesitate to recommend anything specifically,
as it's such a personal choice. And as I said earlier, what works
for one person may not work for the next. So suffice it to say
that this is an option that you can investigate on your own. I
just want to make you aware of all options and I'm not really
endorsing one over another. I do recommend that you don't
schedule things down to the last minute. For example, if you
need to use the toilet every 3 hours, then don't schedule a 2.5
hour flight, in hopes you will be able to use the terminal
bathroom in plenty of time. Flights are often late or delayed,
and sometimes it does take a long time to deplane. Finally, if
you do cut it a bit close, it never hurts to wear a diaper for extra
protection. I know it seems rather an archaic suggestion, but
the extra protection may come in handy. And if you plan to go
the diaper route, consider wearing 2 for extra protection, as
leakage is a common problem.

Getting Off the Airplane—You would think that getting off the plane should be a piece of cake, but here's another area where problems can develop. To nip things in the bud, remember to remind the flight attendant that you will need your wheelchair brought to the gate when you land. This should be done about 30 minutes before landing, well before the flight attendants are busy scurrying through the cabin making last minute pre-landing preparations. One good method is to make friends with a particular flight attendant. Introduce yourself to that flight attendant and learn their name too. Use their name during the flight. Then when you are ready to land, remind that flight attendant about your wheelchair. When you call the flight attendant by name, it puts more of a responsibility on them to follow through with your request. They realize you know their name, and if something goes wrong, they know they will be held personally responsible.

Now, if you need an aisle chair to disembark, you must wait until the rest of the passengers deplane. At that point the aisle chair will be brought to you, and you will be wheeled to the aircraft door, where your own wheelchair will be waiting for you. That's how it's supposed to work, but in practice sometimes it doesn't go that smoothly. I've received countess reports from people who waited an inordinate amount of time on an empty airplane. They waited for somebody to bring them an aisle chair, or for their own wheelchair to be brought up from the baggage compartment. Sometimes the baggage handlers get confused and send the wheelchair to the baggage area, even thought it has a gate tag. There is really no excuse for people having to wait this long to deplane, but it does happen. So, don't plan your connections too tightly, and do hold the airline responsible if you miss your flight. Additionally, take nonstop direct flights whenever possible. I've heard a few creative solutions to the deplaning problem but the best suggestion comes from my friend Dan. He takes his cell phone with him, calls the airline from his seat, and asks to speak to the CRO whenever there is a long delay in deplaning. Does it work? Well, it does seem to get some prompt action, but it really does nothing to solve the big problem. Hopefully the airlines will find a solution, but for now don't be surprised if you encounter a delay in getting off the plane.

CRO—I've already mentioned the Complaints Resolution Office (CRO) a few times in this chapter, so by now you should know this is the person you need to contact if you reach an impasse with front line personnel. The CRO is a problem solver, and is specifically educated on traveler's rights and airline responsibilities under the ACAA. All US airlines are required to have a CRO on duty 24 hours a day, so if you encounter a problem at any stage of game, from reservations to deplaning, this is the person to contact.

Of course, as I pointed out earlier, it really helps to know your rights when talking to the CRO. In other words, don't misquote the law and demand bulkhead seating or a first class upgrade. The CRO will help you resolve access problems, and ultimately get you the services you need, and are entitled to under the law. But, knowing the law is the first and all important step in advocating for yourself. On the other hand, if the airline personnel want you to transfer to an airline wheelchair at check-in, this is a good time to contact the CRO. The law is on your side, and the CRO will help to enforce it.

As far as air travel goes, the best survival tactic is to try and prevent problems before they happen. Of course, there are a lot of unknown variables that factor into the accessibility equation, but you're ahead of the game if you confirm and reconfirm all your travel arrangements. I know this is a time consuming process, and may people think it's an unfair burden to put on travelers with disabilities; but in reality it's the best way to head off potential disasters and help things go smoothly. If you want to make a political statement, then go ahead and leave things to chance; but, if you actually want to take a vacation, remember to confirm and reconfirm all your travel arrangements. You can never be too careful, especially where access is concerned.

2 | On A Wing And A Prayer

Protecting Your Equipment

Getting to your holiday destination with a minimum of muss and fuss can sometimes be a challenge; however, getting your wheelchair or scooter to that same destination, in one piece, can be an even greater chore. Remember, no matter how hard travel is on people, it can be even harder on assistive devices. Generally speaking, passengers aren't stripped of their clothing and thrown into the cargo bin; a fate which many wheelchairs and scooters must routinely endure. Unfortunately, equipment damage is still a top ranked problem for wheelers; but, don't throw in the towel yet, as it's still possible to get your equipment to your final destination relatively unscathed. Of course, as with all aspects of travel, it does take a bit of planning and prepara-tion. Although the whole process may seem rather daunting at first, after a few trips you'll have it down to a science, and then you'll be ready for just about anything.

Before we get into the nuts and bolts here (literally), I must share an anecdote with you. This unfortunate travel tale comes from a reader named Dan. It's about his first air travel experience as a wheeler, and it definitely gets my vote as the ultimate in "wheelchair damage" stories. Now, Dan uses a power wheelchair with gel cell batteries, and even though he could have gate-checked his wheelchair, he relented at check-in and transferred to an airport wheelchair. His plane was then delayed due to weather, and he ended up spending an extra hour in the uncomfortable airport wheelchair. But Dan saw past the pain, as he was really looking forward to his vacation. He remained optimistic. To his delight, when boarding time came things went like clockwork. Dan was boarded first, he had no problems with the aisle chair, and his reserved seat had a moveable armrest. Things couldn't have gone any better. Dan sat back, and stared out the window while the other passengers boarded. He was in a semi-dream state when he noticed an unusual object out on the tarmac. Upon closer examination, it appeared to be his wheelchair. Just as he was about to call the flight attendant, he noticed another object approaching the wheelchair; a 747 backing up out of the gate. He sat there speechless, as he watched the jumbo jet crush his wheelchair. Ultimately he canceled his trip. On the positive side, this incident happened while he was at home, rather than while he was on the road.

Fortunately Dan's experience is not the norm, but it does illustrate the importance of staying in your own wheelchair as long as possible. In Dan's case the cargo handlers forgot to move Dan's wheelchair off the tarmac when his flight was delayed. In theory, if Dan had stayed in his own wheelchair up to the aircraft door, it would have been taken directly to the cargo bin, instead of sitting on the tarmac. Today, Dan always turns down the airport wheelchair, no matter how hard the check-in agent tries to convince him otherwise.

Dan's story pretty much represents the worst case scenario. The only thing I can ever imagine being worse, is actually being in your wheelchair when a 747 backs over it. So, when you encounter equipment damage problems, think about Dan. You'll be able to take some comfort in the fact that no matter how bad things are, at least a jumbo jet didn't roll over your wheelchair.

Avoid The Cargo Bin—The best way to protect your assistive device from damage (short of staying home) is to keep it out of the cargo bin. Let's look at things realistically. When you relinquish your wheelchair to the baggage handler, it really is a crap shoot. Face it, nobody is going to take the same care with your wheelchair that you do; and most certainly not some baggage handler who has a schedule to keep. So where does that leave you? Well, some people have a choice in these matters, so the first step is to learn what can be carried in the passenger compartment, and what has to go in the cargo bin.

You can take canes and crutches on board most aircraft. You have to stow these items for takeoff and landing (for safety reasons), but you can get a flight attendant to retrieve them after you are airborne. You should make it a point to get your assistive device back after takeoff, as you will most likely need it if you want to move about the cabin. Additionally, if there were an emergency, it would be a good idea to have it with you.

Walkers can sometimes be carried in the passenger compartment, depending on the dimensions of the walker and the availability of an onboard closet. Here's where knowing the dimensions of the onboard closet comes in handy, as you will then be able to determine if you walker will fit. Frankly, walkers don't fare very well in the cargo bin, so it wouldn't be a bad idea to invest in a folding walker that fits in the onboard closet. Some manual wheelchairs will also fit in the onboard closet, depending on the size of the wheelchair and the dimensions of the onboard closet. Remember to take advantage of the preboarding privilege, as your assistive device gets priority space in the onboard closet only if you preboard the aircraft. Additionally, remember that the onboard closet is not large enough for two wheelchairs, so if you travel with another wheeler, one wheelchair will end up in the cargo bin.

Another solution is to invest in a folding power wheelchair or scooter. This is not really a good option for full time wheelchair or scooter users, as the products on the market today lack the "pep" that wheelers are used to. However, if you need a wheelchair only for distance, this may be a good solution. Amigo Mobility manufactures a lightweight folding scooter, the TravelMate, which weighs only 61 pounds (with the battery pack.) Compact Mobility's Gypsy scooter folds down to fit into most car trunks, yet carries up to 225 pounds. And Wheelchair Carrier, Inc. manufactures a unique folding power wheelchair, the Roamer Riding Chair. Again, all of these devices are best suited for slow walkers, rather than full time wheelchair users. Additionally when you take any assistive device onboard an aircraft, remember it is not counted as carry-on luggage.

Of course if you can't keep your wheelchair out of the cargo bin, it's a good idea to travel with an older wheelchair (if you have one). Some people travel with their old "backup" wheelchair. Another good solution is to rent a wheelchair or scooter at your destination. Obviously this option only works for people who use a wheelchair or scooter for distance, but it is something to consider. Scoot Around North America can arrange for the rental of assistive devices throughout the US and on most cruise ships. There is a premium fee charged for this type of rental, because Scoot Around North America acts as the agent. Alternatively, a more economical solution is to the make the rental arrangements directly with a medical supply company at your destination.

Protection—Sometimes, there is just no way to keep your assistive device out of the cargo bin; but, fear not, as a little preparation (and a few techniques) will help you protect you equipment. As I pointed out earlier, the best strategy is to stay in your own chair as long as possible (remember Dan). If your chair has gel cell batteries this is pretty easy, because these batteries don't have to be removed and packed separately. Gel cell batteries are disconnected, and the terminals are wrapped, which is a fairly simple procedure. On the other hand, if your wheelchair doesn't have gel cell batteries, the entire battery is removed and packed in a protective container. This can be a time consuming procedure. You might want to consider changing to gel cell batteries, if they are compatible with your wheelchair. This simple change will save you a lot of time and trouble. You will be asked about the specifics of your batteries when you check in for your flight. If you have gel cell batteries, make sure they are clearly marked, so they won't be inadvertently removed. If you don't have any labeling on your batteries, check with a local medical supply house, as they usually carry labels that are appropriate.

Many wheelchairs can be transported in the cargo bin without being disassembled, but that of course also depends on the aircraft type. Here's where knowing the dimensions of the aircraft, especially the width of the cargo door, comes in handy. For example let's compare two aircraft; the EMB 145 which has 50 seats, and the ATR 42-500 which has 46 seats. Although both aircraft have approximately the same passenger capacity, the dimensions of their cargo doors vary drastically. The EMB 145 has a 39 inch wide cargo door, while the ATR 42-500 has a 54 inch wide cargo door. So, the EMB 145 might not be the ideal choice for a large wheelchair. Even if your only choice was the EMB 145 aircraft, it would help to know, in advance, that you wheelchair was going to be disassembled for transport. This knowledge also gives you the flexibility to shop around and perhaps find a larger aircraft. Sometimes this is the best bet, even if you have to drive to another gateway city.

One of the best things you can do to protect your assistive device is to attach assembly and disassembly directions to your wheelchair or scooter. This sounds like a fairly simple task; however, many people overlook it because they assume that their assistive device will not be disassembled for transport. True, it may not be required to be disassembled under ideal conditions, however it never hurts to have instructions attached. You are not encouraging baggage handlers to disassemble your assistive device by attaching instructions; you are merely giving them the proper instructions should it become necessary. Actually, most baggage handlers prefer not to disassemble assistive devices, as it's just more work for them. But, sometimes due to the volume of cargo, it is necessary, even on the most accessible aircraft.

Instructions should be written clearly and simply in both English and Spanish. If possible, also use numbered illustrations or simple drawings to illustrate the assemble/disassembly procedure. Laminate the instructions and attach them securely to your assistive device. Of course it also helps to talk to the baggage handlers to tell them exactly how to handle your chair; however, this is not always possible. Clear assembly/disassembly instructions will help protect your assistive device. Many people even leave these instructions attached to their wheelchair or scooter all the time, as it saves preparation time when it's time to travel.

Remove any loose or protruding parts from your wheelchair or scooter. This includes items like mirrors, cushions, and leg rests. Put them in a duffel bag and carry them on the aircraft. Do not check them!! Wheelchair parts fall under the category of assistive devices and are not counted as carry-on luggage. Remember, something may be piled on top of your wheelchair in the cargo bin. If your wheelchair or scooter becomes a projectile object, loose or protruding parts may break upon impact. Additionally, remember to let a bit of air out of your tires and to carry on all gel cushions. Most cargo bins are not pressurized. You will also need to protect your joystick, if it's not possible to easily remove it. A plastic cup and packing tape works well for this purpose.

Many people come up with creative ways to protect their wheelchairs during transit. My friend Karen devised the following cheap and easy technique. "I travel fairly often and use an electric wheelchair. I carry on all removable parts, and wrap the entire base of the chair with plastic cling wrap. This helps prevent scratches and dings. It also encapsulates the wires so nothing gets unplugged." I like Karen's method. It's simple, and the only out-of-pocket expense is for a roll or two of plastic cling wrap.

Says frequent-flyer, Mike "I've found that bubble wrap (which you can buy at an office supply store) works well in protecting my wheelchair from damage. I just take some to the airport with me and then before I turn my wheelchair over to the airline I pad the areas most likely to sustain damage. I also take some tape with me, so I can secure the bubble wrap. So far, so good."

Other travelers go a bit farther (and spend a bit more money), in their quest to limit wheelchair damage. In fact Gloria even went as far as to build her own transport crate. "I was tired of the airlines damaging my son's wheelchair, so I had a crate building company build a protective container for transport. They built a crate that has 4 locking caster wheels, handles, and a side door with a moveable ramp. All the major airlines have accepted the crate so far, although I do have to make advance arrangements for it. Now, the crate comes back beat up, but the wheelchair remains undamaged."

Gloria is on the right track, in fact there is even a company that sells protective containers for wheelchair air transport. The Haseltine Corporation manufactures and sells such protective containers, which are constructed out of rigid molded plastic. There are 2 models of the Haseltine Flyer, one for folding manual wheelchairs and another for power wheelchairs and scooters. Model "504-A" is designed for folding wheelchairs and consists of a polyethylene container with foam padding and internal straps to hold accessories in place. It is also available with wheels. The larger "504-C" model is designed for rigid motorized chairs and scooters. The Haseltine Flyers are priced between $300-$800, depending on the model. The down-side is that you have to arrange for storage of the container at your destination. Contact your airline in advance for more information on this matter. The Haseltine containers have been tested by several airlines, but so far no airline has purchased any. On the other hand, travelers are starting to realize the advantages of the Haseltine Flyer, and so far, they have been the primary market. We can only hope that the airlines will one day follow suit.

And finally, do remember to take a tool kit of basic tools with you when you travel. You will need these to prepare your assistive device for transport. Additionally, a tool kit will enable you to make quick repairs on the road, which will save you time and money. Your tool kit should include items such as a small screwdriver with interchangeable bits, a crescent wrench, a couple of Allen wrenches, a small roll of electrical tape, a few lengths of electrical wire, an assortment of electrical connectors, and a variety of nuts, bolts and washers. Your own tool kit will of course depend on your particular equipment, but do remember to carry it in your carry-on bag. Never check it! Additionally, if you use a scooter, don't forget to pack a spare key in your emergency tool kit. You never know when you will need it.

When Protection Isn't Enough—Sometimes, no matter how hard you try, the inevitable happens. Your wheelchair is damaged in transit. Unfortunately it happens, so you do need to be prepared for it. The first thing you should do is learn what the ACAA says about airline liability for damage to assistive devices.

The ACAA originally limited airline liability for damage to assistive devices to $2500. Due to public pressure, and the rising incidence of wheelchair damage by the airlines, the Department of Transportation (DOT) eliminated this cap on Aug. 2, 1999. The new rule governing airline damage to assistive devices became effective on September 1, 1999.

The new rule lifted the previous cap, established guidelines for valuation, and permitted recovery for consequential damages. Under the new rule, airlines are responsible for all repairs to damaged devices; however, if the devices are lost or damaged beyond repair, the airlines are only responsible for the original purchase price. For example, if you paid $3000 for your wheelchair 10 years ago, but it would cost $5500 to replace it today; you can only expect to recover the original purchase price ($3000) if your wheelchair is damaged beyond repair. Your are responsible for the additional $2500 it would cost to replace your wheelchair.

Travelers are cautioned to know both the purchase price and the replacement cost of their assistive devices; and to be aware of the difference between these two figures. If the difference is substantial, you may want to carry additional insurance with a high deductible to cover this gap.

Airlines are also required to pay for consequential damages, such as wheelchair rental, and unrefundable tickets, tours or deposits. It is highly probable that many early claims for consequential damages will be settled in court, thus setting a precedent. Please be aware that these rules only apply to US based carriers. The current compensation cap for international flights is still $9.07/LB (covered under the Warsaw Convention). Know your rights and the value of your equipment before you fly, and make sure you have adequate insurance coverage to cover your assistive devices.

It's also important to remember to report any damage to your wheelchair or scooter immediately. In most cases this means before you leave the airport. Admittedly some internal damage is hard to detect immediately, but it is important to report it as soon as you become aware of it. Even though you may be in the middle of a holiday, you need to take time out to file a claim with the airline if you expect to recover your damages. The airline may deny a claim if they feel it is not filed in a timely manner. Additionally, under the ACAA, airlines are not required to respond to complaints that are more than 45 days old.

Again, this seems like a very simple task, but it amazes me how many people don't understand the importance of timeliness in this matter. For example one lady I talked to at a health fair last year told me about some damage done to her scooter on a "recent" airline flight. When I inquired as to her definition of "recent", she matter-of-factly replied, "About eight months ago. Should I file a claim?" Unfortunately this is not an isolated incident. If you had an automobile accident and you waited eight months to report the damage, do you think your insurance company would pay the claim? Most likely they wouldn't. And neither will the airlines. Report all damage, (no matter how small it seems) immediately.

Finally, no matter how bad things seem, even if your wheelchair is returned to you in pieces, don't panic. I know this is easier said than done, but I would like to illustrate the importance of this point with a story about my friend John. John is a pretty well seasoned traveler, but every now and then life throws him a few curves. On a recent trip to the Bahamas John's wheelchair was literally returned to him in pieces. John relates his humbling experience, "First they brought out the frame, then they kept bringing out smaller and smaller pieces. I didn't even know my wheelchair had that many pieces. Actually I didn't care about the wheelchair, as I travel with my old backup klunker; but I didn't want to ruin my long-anticipated holiday. I just blew a fuse and started cussing and screaming. I was quite a sight, right there in the middle of the airport. The embarrassing thing was that the baggage handler had my wheelchair back together in about 2 minutes. Apparently this was standard procedure. I wheeled out with my tail tucked between my legs." On the positive side, he adds, "I didn't even think about renting a car there. I figured if they could assemble my wheelchair that quickly, they could do wonders stripping a car."

Loaners—Although your tool kit will allow you to make quick repairs on the road, if you wheelchair is badly damaged you will have to relinquish it while it is being repaired. In the interim you will need an appropriate loaner. But what is an appropriate loaner? That depends on who you ask, as some airline personnel have an interesting definition of "appropriate." It's not that they are trying to pull a fast one on you, it's just that they really don't understand the difference between your Quickie and their E&J airport wheelchair.

So, here's where a little patience comes in. Again, this is easier said than done, especially if you are tired and cranky (not to mention mad.) In order to advocate for yourself and to get what you define as an appropriate loaner wheelchair, you need to calmly explain the facts of life to the airline personnel assigned to help you. You may even have to do this more than once, to a supervisor or another clerk. No matter how frustrating this is, it's the only way to get a wheelchair that will adequately suit your needs. If you have a highly specialized chair, you might even do some advance research, and find an appropriate rental outlet at your destination (just in case.) Whatever happens, keep your temper, and remember that the airlines are responsible for providing you with an appropriate loaner chair. In other words, if their E&J won't suit your needs, they have to foot the bill for an appropriate rental. Keep talking till they get it right.

Finally, if you don't get satisfaction from talking with front line personnel, ask to speak to the Complaints Resolution Officer (CRO). The CRO will help you get the services you are entitled to, including an appropriate loaner chair.

3 | Up, Up And Away

Beyond Wheelchairs

"I use therapeutic oxygen. Is it possible for me to travel by air?"

"I need to remain in a reclining position? What are my options for air travel?"

"I use a ventilator and want to travel by air. Is this possible? What advance arrangements do I need to make?"

"I've never traveled by air with my service animal. What can I expect? What are my rights?"

People approach me with questions like these all the time. Admittedly there are no pat answers to these questions; in fact, the answers are usually dependent upon the individual circumstances of the traveler. These topics all fall into what I call the "beyond wheelchairs" category of air travel. In some instances, such as stretcher travel, special medical clearance is required. In other instances, such as travel with a service animal, travelers merely need to learn the rules and regulations, so they know what to expect. In all instances, in-depth research is usually required. So, let's take a look at some of these "special" cases.

To be quite honest, I really dislike the word "special," as it carries such bad connotations. It implies segregation, in this era of inclusion. Years ago people were segregated into special programs, while today everybody is included in the same accessible program. Personal feelings aside, many airlines insist on using this archaic term to describe certain services or departments. For example, when you need information about travel with therapeutic oxygen, you usually contact the special services department. So, I hesitantly use the term "special," here, and more importantly, I use it only to direct you to the most appropriate airline department.

Oxygen—Travel with therapeutic oxygen is not specifically covered under the Air Carriers Access Act (ACAA). By this I mean, US airlines are not required to provide therapeutic oxygen services to their passengers. Each airline sets its own policy regarding therapeutic oxygen services. Currently, America West and Southwest Airlines do not accept passengers who travel with therapeutic oxygen. This exclusion is well within their legal rights, as travel with therapeutic oxygen is considered a safety issue, and as such it is regulated by the Federal Aviation Administration (FAA). Of course this statement usually prompts a lively discourse from therapeutic oxygen users.

The usual argument presented by therapeutic oxygen users is that their equipment is very safe, and as such it should be allowed on all commercial aircraft. Well, there are two reasons the FAA considers therapeutic oxygen a safety issue. First, even though most people maintain their equipment in excellent working order, you never know when somebody could unintentionally bring damaged equipment on board. And second, an oxygen cylinder is an excellent place to conceal an explosive device; a device which could potentially go undetected by security. Plus, to be honest, some airlines just don't want to take the time to train their personnel or to make the proper arrangements. Either way, the airlines are allowed to set their own policies on this matter, so your only choice is to deal with an airline that does provide therapeutic oxygen services. Before you decide which airline to travel with, call around and ask them all about their specific policies and procedures regarding therapeutic oxygen.

Procedures vary between carriers, and they can change at any time. Please note that many non-US carriers also accept passengers who use therapeutic oxygen.

Although different airlines have different procedures regarding therapeutic oxygen, they all prohibit passengers from using their own equipment on board. Passengers must use airline supplied oxygen. There is a charge for this service, and it usually runs between $50-$150 per flight leg. A flight leg is defined as the time between one takeoff and one landing, so try and book a non-stop direct flight whenever possible. Most insurance policies do not cover in-flight oxygen, so check with your insurance carrier in advance. Even if your insurance carrier does cover in-flight oxygen; remember, airlines require payment in advance and they won't accept an insurance assignment. You will have to pay the cost up front, and seek reimbursement from your insurance company.

All US airlines require a doctor's statement from passengers who intend to travel with therapeutic oxygen. Some airlines require the doctor to fill out specific forms, while others ask for a prescription. When making your travel arrangements make sure and ask what kind of oxygen equipment is provided. Some airlines provide flow meters that can be adjusted from 2-8 liters, while others have flow meters with a low (2l) and a high (4l) setting. Ask the airline if you need to bring your own mask or cannula. Some airlines provide them and some don't. It's also a good idea to take some empty tanks with you, so you can have them refilled at your destination. Airlines will allow you to carry empty tanks, but you must check them with your baggage. You cannot carry them on board the aircraft with you.

You will also need to make arrangements for oxygen services at your destination. Check with the airport to make sure they allow oxygen use in the terminal. Then, check with your local oxygen supplier to see if they are affiliated with a national chain that can provide service to you at your destination. You will have to have the oxygen delivered to the airport, as you cannot use the in-flight oxygen in the terminal. Alternatively you can have a friend or relative meet you at the airport with your oxygen supplies.

The price for airport delivery of oxygen varies, however since it's a labor intensive service, it's cheaper during regular business hours. You will pay a premium price for this service on weekends and in the evenings, so try and time your arrival accordingly. Location also makes a difference, as oxygen services are just cheaper at certain airports. For example, you will pay bargain prices for oxygen at Philadelphia, Denver and Miami airports; but oxygen services at Boston, Washington DC (Dulles) and Minneapolis airports are among the most expensive in the nation. In any case, it never hurts to call more than one supplier to get a competitive price. Many oxygen suppliers will not accept an insurance assignment for oxygen delivered to the airport, so be prepared to pay cash. You will also have to arrange for airport oxygen at your connecting airport, if you cannot arrange a direct flight.

Finding an oxygen provider outside of the US, may be a little more difficult. Oxygen prescriptions written by US doctors are not valid outside of the US. Check with a foreign oxygen supplier to see if you need a prescription. If you do, sometimes the best bet is to work with a US provider that has contracts with foreign oxygen providers. You local oxygen supplier should be able to give you some good resources.

Another good resource for all therapeutic oxygen users is *Breathin' Easy*, by Jerry Gorby. Published annually, this handy guide includes over 2,500 updated listings for oxygen outlets in more than 100 countries. It also includes helpful tips for traveling by air, sea or land with therapeutic oxygen.

The American Lung Association of San Diego and Imperial Counties publishes a good travel guide for people with chronic breathing problems. Filled with checklists, travel tips and worldwide resources, the *Better Breathers Traveler* offers travel strategies for people with asthma, allergies, COPD or other breathing difficulties. Contact the American Lung Association of San Diego and Imperial Counties for pricing and ordering information.

Ventilators—Most US air carriers accept vent-users as passengers; however only a few airlines provide onboard electricity for medical equipment. As you may have guessed, policies and procedures vary from airline to airline. Additionally the availability of onboard electricity is also dependent on the aircraft type. There are a lot of restrictions associated with the use of onboard electricity for medical equipment. Airline policies on this subject change frequently; so even if you travel often, check around with the different carriers for policy updates. Here's what a few US carriers recently had to say about their current policies.

Northwest Airlines Generally speaking, ventilators can be plugged into the onboard electrical system, provided they are compatible and do not interfere with the aircraft's communication and navigation systems.

Delta Air Lines Ventilators may be used on flights that have onboard electrical outlets. However these outlets are only at certain seat locations on some aircraft types, and the customer is responsible for providing any adapters.

United Airlines A number of the more common battery powered devices are pre-approved for acceptance. All others must be cleared by United's medical and engineering staff. Passengers cannot "plug in" equipment to the onboard power, but United can provide a special electrical hook up for some devices.

It goes without saying that you need to make your arrangements well in advance, and reconfirm all arrangements at least 48 hours prior to travel. Always carry a backup battery and charger with you, because even if onboard power is available it can be dependent on the operational needs of the aircraft. Additionally, onboard electrical power is subject to power surges during hookup and disconnection from ground power.

Check around with the various carriers to see if they can provide onboard electricity for your equipment. If not, you might want to consider traveling under battery power. This option obviously depends on your equipment and on the length of your flight. It's not a possibility for everyone, but it may be worth your consideration.

If you do travel under battery power, take a backup battery and a charger with you on board the aircraft. That way, if you run low on battery power, (and happen to be on the ground) you can have somebody get off the plane and recharge one battery for you. This method is especially useful if there is a delay in deplaning. Above all, know the limitations of your equipment and don't plan things too tight. Always allow for some delays when making your calculations.

Make sure your equipment has gel cell batteries and that they are clearly marked. Wet cell batteries are not allowed on board the aircraft. Your equipment must fit under the seat in front of you. If your equipment does not fit in this area, you may strap it to an adjoining seat; however, you will have to purchase the adjoining seat if you go this route. There are no additional or special seating options for passengers who travel with a ventilator. You can always request an upgrade, but in this day and age upgrades usually go to the top echelon of frequent flyers. Still, it never hurts to ask, but don't depend on it. I know some vent-users who insist that they need to be seated in the first row of first class (when traveling on an economy class ticket). After a heated argument with ground personnel, they usually end up in coach. Remember, the airlines are not required by law to upgrade you, so if you request an upgrade, keep in mind that it's request, not a demand.

While in the terminal, keep your ventilator plugged into a wall receptacle until the last possible moment, so your battery will have a 100% charge when you board the aircraft. Take along a 25-50 foot extension cord and an adapter which converts a three pronged plug into as two pronged plug. The control panels at the end of most jetways have an AC plug, so keep this in mind for emergency situations. Keep an eye open for these AC plugs when you board the plane, just in case there is a lengthy delay in boarding.

Speaking of delays, what do you do if you experience a long delay on the tarmac? Well, first off if you give yourself some extra time, you won't have this problem under usual circumstances. But then there are unusual circumstances, which are either weather or traffic related. So, what do you do if you end up sitting on the tarmac for an hour, or more? Experienced vent-users say the best thing to do is to calmly explain the situation to the flight attendant. You need to stress that it is a matter of life and death, not merely a comfort matter. As silly as this sounds, some people just don't understand the concept of a ventilator. Be patient, and if you efforts fail ask to speak to the CRO by radio.

Although it's not travel specific, a good resource for vent-users is the International Ventilator Users Network (IVUN). IVUN is a worldwide network of ventilator users and health professionals experienced in and committed to home care and long-term mechanical ventilation. IVUN publishes *IVUN News*, a quarterly newsletter, offering articles on family adjustments, equipment, techniques, medical topics, ethical issues, travel, and resources.

Stretchers—Although most people consider stretcher travel a medical necessity rather than an vacation option; it may be the ideal solution if you are not able to sit upright or if your require additional head and neck support. To be clear here, I'm not talking about travel by a private air ambulance, but stretcher travel on a commercial air carrier. Many people don't even know this option is available, and although it's more costly than standard airfare, it's still much cheaper than an air ambulance.

Before you decide to travel by stretcher on a commercial airline, you should first rule out the possibility of first class travel. Although seat comfort varies from carrier to carrier, a first class seat might do the trick. The drawback to a first class seat is that it may not offer the needed head and neck support. There is no airline equipment which offers additional neck support, but I've seen some homemade devices created by a few enterprising folks. They all center around a neck pillow and chest straps. Additionally, even though first class seating offers more reclining room, all seats must be in an upright position for takeoff and landing. So, depending on your needs, this may work for you. It is the cheaper option, so it is worth ruling out before you decide to go the stretcher route.

Currently Northwest Airlines is the only US airline that provides stretcher service for people who must remain in a reclining position during the flight. Stretcher service is only available on select aircraft, including the Airbus 320, Boeing 757, Boeing 727-200, Boeing 747-200, 747-400, McDonnell Douglas DC-10-30 and DC-10-40 aircraft. The stretcher can hold up to 250 pounds, and can accommodate a person up to 6'2". It is carried in the coach passenger compartment, and placement is dependent upon the aircraft configuration. Existing seats are folded down and a stretcher frame is installed.

Pricing for stretcher travel is dependent upon both the aircraft and the destination. Passengers must also be delivered and picked up by ambulance. The ambulance fees are not included in the pricing below. Passengers must arrange for ambulance transport separately. Here's a breakdown of the current pricing for stretcher travel on Northwest Airlines.

> **Domestic-A320/727/757:** Four times the full first class fare **DC-10, 747-200, 747-400:** Six times the full coach fare
> **Transatlantic-DC-10/747-200/747-200:** Seven times the unrestricted economy fare
> **Transpacific-DC-10/747-200/747-200:** Nine times the unrestricted economy fare

Under the ACAA, airlines may require a medical certificate from passengers who travel by stretcher. Northwest Airlines requires such documentation. The medical certificate is merely a written statement from the passenger's physician stating that the passenger is capable of completing the flight safely. The medical certificate should state that no extraordinary medical assistance will be required during the flight. Northwest Airlines also requires stretcher passengers to sign a liability release prior to departure. All stretcher passengers are required to travel with an attendant or companion who can see to their needs during the flight. This is also permitted under the ACAA.

Reservations for stretcher travel must be made at least 48 hours in advance. Stretcher requests may be made through Northwest's Domestic Reservations at 1-800-225-2525 or International Reservations at 1-800-447-4747. Northwest Airlines also has a helpful brochure, "Air Travel for People with Disabilities", which is available by calling 800-358-3100.

Service Animals—By now, I'm sure you've heard the tale about the two ladies who boarded a US Air flight with their 350 pound pig in tow. They claimed porky was a service animal, and US Air employees bought their story and allowed the pig to ride in the first class cabin. Although much confusion surrounds the exact events that transpired during the flight, everybody agrees that the pig defecated on the jetway.

So, was the pig a service animal as defined under the ACAA? No, it wasn't. And not because it was a pig, or because it reportedly took four people to wheel it aboard the aircraft. It's not considered a service animal because it did not behave appropriately on board the aircraft. What is appropriate behavior? Well, it isn't (as one passenger reported) "running loose through the aircraft, and squealing loudly". Enough of the fairy tales. Let's look at what the ACAA has to say regarding real service animals.

Under the ACAA, US airlines must allow service animals to accompany any qualified person with a disability on board the aircraft. This applies to any guide dog, signal dog or any other animal trained to provide assistance to a person with a disability. This rule only applies to service animals while they are traveling with a person with a disability. For example if a non-disabled animal trainer needed to transport a service animal by air, the service animal would be subject to the airline's general regulations regarding the carriage of animals. In other words, the service animal would not necessarily have the right to accompany the trainer in the cabin.

Assuming that the service animal is traveling with a person with a disability, the service animal is allowed to accompany that individual everywhere on the aircraft. People who travel with a service animal are entitled to bulkhead seating if they desire, however they are not required to sit in the bulkhead section. They may choose a non-bulkhead seat if they prefer. The service animal must not obstruct the aisle or any other area required by the FAA safety rules to remain unobstructed. If there is no space in the cabin that can accommodate the animal without causing such an obstruction, the animal is not permitted to travel in the cabin. Most of the time service animals have no problems traveling on commercial air carriers. The exception might be on some smaller aircraft, where there may not be enough room for the animal to sit at the owner's feet without protruding out into the aisle. If a small aircraft is your only choice, ask for the seating dimensions (before you make your reservations) so you can determine if there is enough room for your service animal to sit at your feet.

Of course it is the owner's responsibility to make sure that their animal acts appropriately while on the aircraft. This is usually not much of a problem, as service animals are highly trained to act appropriately in public situations. If the service animal exhibits inappropriate behavior such as growling, barking or running up and down the aisle, the airlines are not required to treat it as a service animal. Airline personnel are trained to first try and mitigate the effects of such behavior. For example, if a service animal barks, they might suggest a muzzle to try and solve the problem. It mitigation doesn't work, they do have the right to require that the service animal travel in the cargo bin.

Generally speaking, a properly trained service animal should have no problems traveling on a commercial carrier.

One subject that comes up a lot when talking about service animals and air travel is cleaning and damage fees. Are they legal? The ACAA prohibits special charges such as deposits or surcharges for accommodations made for passengers with a disability. However an airline can charge a passenger with a disability for damage done by their service animal, as long as it's the policy of the airline to charge non-disabled passengers for the same type of damage. For example, if the airline regularly charges non-disabled passengers for cleaning and repair to damaged seats; they can also charge a person traveling with a service animal for similar damages. Again, a properly trained service animal should have no problems, but it's always a good idea to know your rights.

Of course bathroom facilities are always a matter of concern, and the obvious question is how do you handle this situation while you are en route with your service animal. I mean, finding an accessible bathroom is one thing, but finding an area for your pooch to do his business is another matter entirely. Well, according to my well traveled friend Connie, there is a definite procedure. "Basically you have to take connecting flights, and leave enough time in between flights for a doggy pit stop. The airline needs to be advised that you are traveling with a service animal and that you will need assistance at the connecting airport to walk your dog. There are computer codes the airlines use for passengers traveling with service animals. There isn't a specific code that addresses the doggy potty stop issue, so you need to ask the reservation clerk to note this in the remarks section. Of course you also need to check back to make sure this has been done. Even after all that hassle, sometimes they still don't get it right. Don't panic, just ask to be guided to the appropriate area when you disembark."

And finally, be sure to inquire in advance about any restrictions or special procedures for importing animals at your destination. Some countries impose strict quarantines on incoming animals, and most of these quarantines do not exclude service animals. The US is not free from restrictions either. Hawaii just lifted their strict quarantine in 1998 (actually it's a settlement to a lawsuit); however, Hawaii-bound service animals still face some entry restrictions. The terms of the settlement apply only to residents of the US who have guide dogs trained at schools belonging to the US Council Guide Dog Schools. The settlement allows these animals to enter Hawaii without quarantine, providing they adhere to a required program of vaccinations, exams, titers and microchip identification. For details on the procedures, contact Guide Dog Users Inc., 14311 Astrodome Dr., Silver Springs, MD, 20906 (888) 858-1008.

4 | Getting Around on the Ground

Accessible ground transportation is one of the most important components of any trip; because without it, you can literally fall flat on your face. You can also be stuck at the airport, trapped at your hotel, or segregated and separated from the rest of your party. The availability of accessible ground transportation can literally make or break a trip. It's also one of the major components of seamless travel; a term I coined many years ago while researching a story on San Diego.

Seamless travel is defined as "travel without any gaps in accessible services or facilities." Quite simply it means you can get from the airport, train or bus station to your accessible accommodations. And it means once you get there, you won't have to sit in your hotel room because the tourist attractions or public facilities are not accessible. If you're talking about cruises, seamless travel means that cruise ships, as well as shore excursions, and transfers should all be accessible. Obviously we have a long way to go in making seamless travel a reality; however I believe it's a very viable goal.

Until seamless travel becomes a reality, it pays to investigate your accessible ground transportation options before you leave home. This will not only save you a lot of time and trouble, but in some cases it will also save you money.

Airport Transportation—Since many people travel by air, finding accessible airport transportation is a top priority. Your options vary depending on your destination, and in most cases even on your arrival time. There is some advance research you can do, but it's not a foolproof system. The best advice I can give you is to do your research, know your options and make advance arrangements whenever possible; however, be prepared for unexpected delays.

If you are staying at a hotel, find out if they offer courtesy airport transportation. Under the Americans with Disabilities Act (ADA), hotels that offer courtesy transportation must also provide accessible transportation free of charge. The catch is that most front desk personnel don't know this fact; so, you have to know your rights and learn how to advocate for yourself. I shudder to think how many people are charged for this service because they don't know that it must be provided free of charge. In fact that's exactly what (almost) happened to my friend Dana.

When Dana first made her hotel reservation she inquired about airport transfers. The clerk told her that they did have a courtesy shuttle but it wasn't accessible. Before Dana had a chance to express her disappointment, the clerk chimed in and said he could make arrangements for her with a local accessible transportation company. Dana was relieved that somebody else could take care of the details. The clerk called her back later and told her that everything had been arranged and even gave her a confirmation number. He also told Dana that it would cost $25. At first this seemed fine to Dana. Of course she blew a gasket when I told her that legally the hotel could not charge her for this service. She immediately called the manager and registered a complaint. The manager apologized profusely, and told her that of course there would be no charge for her airport transfers.

Remember, if a property offers free airport transfers, they must also provide accessible airport transfers at no charge. Additionally, they cannot charge guests for this service, even if they have to contract it out. Don't let hotels off the hook on this issue, and if you run into problems (like Dana did), ask to speak to the manager. Management is usually well educated on ADA matters.

Many cab companies now have at least some accessible vehicles in their fleet. Again, if you are staying at a hotel you may be able to glean a little information about the local cab companies from the desk clerk. Call the companies directly and ask if they operate any accessible vehicles. If not, ask if they know of any local companies that do have accessible vehicles. Be sure and specify your needs when talking to a cab company. Some cab companies operate ramp equipped vans, while others consider a cab with a large trunk an accessible vehicle. You may be able to make advance arrangements for an accessible cab. This policy varies, and most companies only accept reservations 24-48 hours in advance.

Some cab companies operate accessible ramp-equipped vans. Pictured here is an accessible taxi in San Francisco.

If a cab won't suit your needs, find out if there are any airport transportation companies that serve the area. Again, some of these companies do have accessible vehicles. The service varies from company to company. The good news about airport transportation companies is that you can always book them in advance. The bad news is that sometimes they show up without the accessible vehicle. My friend John travels with his Hoyer lift, and uses airport transportation companies frequently. There seems to be no consistency in service, as even national companies are locally managed. Sometimes John has a great experience and sometimes it's the pits. The best strategy is to call and reconfirm you reservation at least 24 hours in advance, and of course remind the company that you do need an accessible vehicle.

Public transportation is another option, although I tend to shy away from buses. There's nothing worse than riding on a crowded bus after a long plane trip. Plus, buses are at the mercy of traffic, and if you hit it at the wrong time, a 15 minute trip can turn into a 45 minute ordeal. Find out if there is a local rail or metro station at the airport, and if it stops close to your hotel. Contact the public transportation authority to find out if it is accessible. Many airports have great metro service. I personally recommend taking the metro from Ronald Regan airport in Washington DC. It's convenient, accessible and very affordable. However, If you arrive late at night, I'd stick to private transportation. It's never a good idea to wander around a large city, suitcase in tow, after dark.

Finding accessible airport transportation is sometimes just a matter of whittling down your options. Contact the local Convention and Visitors Bureau (CVB) and find out what airport transportation options exist. Then, inquire directly with the individual providers to find out if they offer any accessible transportation. Most CVBs don't know a lot about accessibility, however they can usually provide you with a long list of transportation providers. Additionally a few CVBs now publish access guides. These access guides describe the accessibility of all tourist services, including airport transportation. Hopefully in the coming years more CVBs will realize the importance of providing accurate access information. Until then, it never hurts to ask.

No matter what type of transportation you choose, it's a good idea to take a cell phone with you when you travel. It comes in handy when you're curbside, waiting for that long-delayed hotel shuttle. It sure beats trekking back to the terminal in search of a phone. Shop around and find a cellular plan that allows you to make long distance calls at no extra charge, and one that doesn't add roam charges for calls made out of the area.

Public Transportation—Most people require some form of transportation once the get to their destination; however, today many travelers rely on public transportation. When choosing your hotel try and find one that is close to many of the attractions you wish to see. Additionally, remember to pick a hotel that is close to the bus and metro stops, as utilizing public transportation will save you money. Of course, you will have to do some pre-trip research to find out what types of accessible public transportation are available.

One of the best resources for accessible transportation is the Project Action Accessible Transportation Database. Created by the Easter Seals Society, this on-line database lists accessible transportation throughout the United States, including taxis, buses, hotel shuttles and airport transportation. There is no charge to access it, and it can be found *www.projectaction.org*. I have to say that this database contains the most accurate information on the subject.

Of course there are a few other accessible transportation guides out there, but I've reviewed most of them and found them all to be lacking in accurate information. Plus, some of them are quite expensive. My advice is to save your money and use the Project Action Database. If you don't have internet access, you can connect to the internet at your local library.

When you search the Project Action Database, you will be able to get contact information for the public transportation authority in your destination city. This is very important information, as you can glean specific access information from the local public transit authority. Of course the volume and detail of the information varies from city to city, but some public transportation authorities even produce access guides. Such is the case with the San Francisco Municipal Railway (Muni), one of the public transportation authorities serving the Bay area. Muni operates the local bus and rail routes and publishes the excellent "Muni Access Guide" which describes their accessible services. Many other public transportation authorities are publishing printed access guides. Again, don't be afraid to ask. Additionally, most public transportation authorities have some sort of access information on their website.

Don't rule out public transportation, as many times it's accessible. The San Diego Trolley (light rail) is pictured here.

Another great resource is the local Center for Independent Living (CIL). These nationwide centers go by a variety of names, Including Independent Living Centers (ILC), Resources for Independent Living (RIL) and Independent Living Resources (ILR). The one thing they all have in common is that they provide resources, advocacy and support for people with disabilities who want to live independently. The focus of each CIL differs, and some are better than others. Still, accessible public transportation is a big issue for people with disabilities, so many CILs have information on this subject. Many people working in the CILs rely on accessible public transportation, so you may get some helpful first-hand information. Again, it depends on the CIL, and in some cases even the contact person. But, it can be a valuable resource, so I encourage people to give it a try whenever possible.

TIRR publishes the most accurate CIL directory, through their Independent Living Research Utilization (ILRU) program. ILRU was established in 1977 to serve as a national center for information, training, research, and technical assistance for independent living. ILRU's Directory of Independent Living Programs is a comprehensive listing of over 400 programs providing independent living services in the US and Canada. The directory costs $10 and can be obtained in many formats. For more information contact TIRR at 713-520-0232 or visit *www.bcm.tmc.edu/ilru/ilru-directory.html*. Please note that TIRR produces the most accurate and updated CIL directory, clearly a bargain for the $10 price.

Rental Vehicles—Admittedly, public transportation is not for everybody; and some people just like the convenience of driving their own vehicle. People that want this convenience can either take their personal vehicle on a road trip, or rent a vehicle at their destination. Either way, it's best to investigate the availability and pricing of parking at your destination before you make this decision. In some cities, like San Francisco, parking is expensive and pretty much non-existent. And although most cities in the US honor placards from other states, New York City is the exception to this rule. Unless you have a local New York City placard, expect to be cited or towed (or both) if you park in a designated accessible space in the Big Apple.

Most rental car agencies offer a variety of adaptive equipment for rental cars. Depending on the location, 24-48 hours notice is required for installation of hand controls and spinner knobs. Since there are a wide variety of manufacturers of adaptive equipment, there can be a bit of confusion when it comes to getting the proper equipment installed. A good tip is to take a picture of the adaptive equipment you need, and then fax or mail a copy of the photo to the rental car agency. That way they will know exactly what you need, and they can give the photo to their mechanic to insure that the proper device is installed. It's always a good idea to deal directly with the local franchise, in order to make sure that your adaptive equipment request is treated appropriately.

Even a simple request like "hand controls" can cause some confusion. Such was the case with my friend Patty, who had driven her own hand control equipped van for many years. Patty is a bilateral above the knee amputee and uses either a manual or power wheelchair when she travels. Since she was traveling with her 13 year old son, she thought it would be a good idea to take her manual wheelchair and rent a Sports Utility Vehicle (SUV) with hand controls. She figured that she could drive the vehicle, while her son could fold up her wheelchair and stow it in the back. Well, in theory it was a great idea, but in practice it didn't work out very well.

When Patty arrived at the rental facility she could not get into the SUV, because the hand controls protruded out near the bottom. Her own hand controls protrude out at the top, allowing her easy access. She ended up renting a more expensive van, because the hand controls just wouldn't work for her. In retrospect, she thinks she could have avoided this situation by asking the rental car company to send her a photo of the hand controls, as she clearly knows what styles will work for her. She also says that renting the SUV wasn't really a good idea, as there really wasn't enough space for her on the drivers side.

It pays to know what vehicle will suit your needs; and then stick to that choice even if a rental agent tries to talk you into an upgrade. Unfortunately, my friend Darryl learned that lesson the hard way. Darryl recounts his rental car experience in Southeastern Maine in the following excerpt from his trip diary. "I reserved a Ford Contour, which would have suited our needs fine; but, I let the Hertz agent talk us into upgrading to a Ford Explorer. As roomy as it looks, the Explorer is really a pretty poor choice for someone in a wheelchair. It was very tight inside, with no maneuvering room. The doors didn't open very wide and the cargo area didn't hold very much. My son's manual wheelchair barely fit in the back, and left little room for anything else. Plus, I can't count the number of times I hit my back on the door trying to help my son transfer. Oh well, live and learn."

There are some limits on what types of services and equipment rental car agencies are required to offer. Title III of the ADA requires rental car companies to remove transportation barriers that prevent persons with disabilities from being able to use rental cars, when doing so is readily achievable. This covers most adaptive equipment like hand controls, and in most cases spinner knobs. Rental car agencies have long held that some types of mounting hardware used to attach spinner knobs can cause damage to steering wheels. According to the Department of Justice, rental car agencies are not required to install spinner knobs if they damage the vehicle. It all boils down to the type of vehicle and mounting hardware, so if you need a spinner knob on a specific vehicle model, make sure and state this at the time you make your reservation. Theoretically, this should give the rental agency time to make alternate arrangements.

Of course the biggest complaint about most rental car agencies is that they do not rent accessible vans. Congress specifically stated in the ADA, that companies are not required to retrofit vehicles by installing hydraulic or other lifts. Moreover, companies who are in the business of renting vehicles are not required to purchase or lease lift-equipped vehicles. A few car agencies do have affiliate agreements with accessible van rental companies, which allows them to provide accessible vans to their customers. The drawback is that these vans are expensive; they average $100 per day. So it never hurts to ask, but remember that rental car agencies are not required to provide accessible vans.

In addition to adaptive equipment, all car rental facilities in the US are required to make their facilities accessible. In fact a May 2000 settlement of Giacopini v. Hertz Corporation, mandates improved access at Hertz facilities. Under the terms of the settlement, Hertz is required to provide accessible transportation (shuttle buses) between airport terminals and Hertz off-site rental facilities. Additionally Hertz must survey and modify all their public facilities to conform with current ADA Accessibility Guidelines (ADAAG). Although this ADA settlement only pertains Hertz facilities, under the ADA all rental car agencies are required to provide this level of access in their US facilities.

Some people who want to skip the fuss and muss at the rental car counter take their own hand controls with them when they travel. I have to say that although this method does appear to streamline the process, there are some definite drawbacks. First off, many car rental companies will not let you install your own hand controls. Furthermore, if you have an accident, and you install your own hand controls, you won't be covered under most insurance policies. Still some people claim that it's the greatest thing since sliced bread. I can't really endorse this method, because it leaves you open for liability in case of an accident; however, if you are going to try it do remember the following story.

My friend Bob always takes his hand controls with him when he travels. In fact, he's really quite smug about it, bragging all the time about how much money he saves, and how he always has the equipment he needs. That is until his recent trip to

London. It seems that Bob forgot that people drive on the "other side of the road" in the UK. Suffice it to say that his US hand controls would not work on the British cars. He ended up renting a very expensive accessible van. Bob's not quite so smug any more. Watch out for the same thing in Australia and New Zealand.

A few words about rental vehicles in Europe. Although practices vary from country to country, with a little research you can find a car rental company that will install hand controls for you. It's usually easier to find a car with hand controls than an accessible van. The most updated resource on adapted rental cars in Europe can be found on the internet at users.actcom.co.il/~swfm/. It's a private website, and includes a lot of Europe resources.

Additionally, don't forget to pack your parking placard, if your travel plans include renting a car in Europe. In 1997 the European Conference of Ministers of Transport (ECMT) passed Resolution No. 97/4, on "Reciprocal Recognition of Parking Badges for Persons with Mobility Handicaps". As of Jan. 1, 1999, travelers from associate countries, including the USA and Canada, are also included in this resolution. The resolution requires permit holders to "display a document that shows the international symbol for persons with disabilities, as well as the name of the holder of the document", in order to receive reciprocal parking privileges in ECMT countries.

Of course another option is to rent a accessible van. For many people this is the only vehicle that will meet their needs, while for others it seems a wasted expense. Basically it's just a matter of personal preference and need. However, it's good to know that there are many companies that specialize in renting accessible vans throughout the world. The best database of accessible rental van companies is on our own Emerging Horizons website at EmergingHorizons.com. Years ago I realized the need for this information, and decided to provide it on-line, as a community service. I do update the website every 2-3 weeks and I'm constantly adding new links to our travel resources. This should be your first stop if you are in search of a rental van.

And finally, if you want to go in style, consider hiring an accessible limousine. Currently this option is only available in Las Vegas, but it's a great way to treat yourself. Bill Bauers designed his limousine with roll-on access and all the creature comforts you come to expect in a limousine. For more information, contact AKA Limousine in Las Vegas at 702-257-7433. Hopefully Bill will be able to expand to other locations soon.

Tour Vehicles—Although technically not ground transportation, many people use city tours for at least a brief overview of their destination. There are all types of city tours, and access varies. The good news is that beginning in Oct. 2001 (for large companies) and in Oct. 2002 (for smaller companies) most bus type tours will be required to offer an accessible option. Of course there are exceptions to this rule, but according to the DOT regulations for over the road buses, tour operators will be required to provide accessible transportation upon 48 hours notice.

For now, it's nice to know that there are some accessible options around the country. I give high marks to San Diego Trolley Tours for purchasing a lift equipped tour vehicle. Their accessible vehicle looks like old fashioned trolley car, with the lift cleverly concealed beneath the vehicle. Advance notice is required to make sure you get a tour on the accessible vehicle, but still they have done a great job making their tours accessible.

Other tour operators have been more imaginative in making their tours accessible. Such is the case of Frances Zeller, owner of Harbor City Tours in Baltimore, MD. Harbor City Tours is a small business, and admittedly their bus is not wheelchair accessible. Still Frances does offer wheelchair-users the option of using their own vehicle for the tour. She provides the guide and they use their own vehicle. Of course this option won't work for everyone, but it's an excellent example of a small business working to make their services accessible.

RVs—Although most people don't really consider RVs ground transportation, some people use them for both transportation and lodging. Many RV-ers consider this lifestyle to be especially conducive to people with disabilities, as you don't have to worry about accessible hotels, restaurants or restrooms. Still, it's not a worry free existence.

RV-ers have to worry about accessible campgrounds and facilities, and of course they have to choose a RV that suits their needs. Since it's a major expense, many experts advise renting a RV before you purchase one. There are a few dealers across the nation (and even around the world) who rent accessible RV's. For a complete list of those dealers check out the travel resources on EmergingHorizons.com.

Another great resource for RV-ers is Hope Syke's "Enabled RV-er" website. Hope's website includes lots of resources about accessible RV-ing, including information about equipment, rights, destinations and resources. You'll also want to sign up for Hope's free monthly e-zine about accessible RV-ing. And if you are a print-only type of person, catch her column in *RV Companion* magazine. Either way, Hope covers all the bases on accessible RV-ing through her well written articles.

5 | We Will Ride

Bus Travel

Although many people tend to discount over-the-road (OTR) bus transportation as a viable leisure travel option; in reality it's one of the only transportation links to many rural US towns. Indeed, it's also a very economical and (sometimes) flexible way to travel. Additionally, it's a great way to see the country while leaving the driving to somebody else. So, what's the scoop on accessible OTR bus transportation in the US? Well, in order to properly answer that question we must first look at the history and events which surround this issue.

History—In truth, the struggle for access to OTR buses predates the passage of the Americans with Disabilities Act (ADA). In fact many grass roots disability activists fought long and hard for the access we enjoy today. At the top of the list of freedom fighters is ADAPT, the granddaddy of the disability rights organizations. Over the past two decades ADAPT has organized demonstrations, educated the public and lobbied legislators to protect the civil rights of people with disabilities. One of those rights includes the right to ride on a bus without being carried on board like a piece of luggage. Besides being very dangerous, this practice is also incredibly degrading.

In 1997, ADAPT members made a series of Greyhound test rides throughout the country. Greyhound refused passage to 32%

of the test riders. Of those who were permitted to ride, 35% were hand carried on and off the bus, and 25% were dropped or otherwise hurt being "helped" on and off the bus. Keep in mind that these test rides were performed after the passage of the ADA, at a time when OTR buses were supposed to be accessible.

Personally I find it ironic that people compare the disability rights movement to the civil rights movement, as unlike Rosa Parks, many of the people fighting for the rights of people with disabilities couldn't even get on board the bus. In any case, ADAPT found the long hard fight, before and after the ADA was passed.

Access to OTR buses was officially mandated in the ADA, however it was still an uphill battle to achieve appropriate (lift) access. The ADA gave OTR bus companies an additional seven years before they had to buy accessible vehicles. Greyhound claimed that it was too expensive to provide lift access to their buses, and that hand carrying non ambulatory passengers on board was an acceptable alternative. Obviously the disability community strongly disagreed with Greyhound's definition of "appropriate" access.

Finally on September 28, 1998 the Access Board published the final guidelines for access to OTR buses. ADAPT won the battle, as among other things, the final rule states that hand carrying passengers on board a bus is not considered appropriate access. Coincidentally, just prior to passage of the final rule, Greyhound replaced a large portion of their fleet with inaccessible buses. This move outraged the disability community and won Greyhound the moniker of "the dirty dog" among disability rights activists.

Furthermore, shortly after the final rule was issued, the American Bus Association sought legal intervention to overturn the rule. The case was originally heard in Washington DC District Court, (American Bus Association, Inc. v. Rodney E. Slater), and was later appealed in Federal Appeals Court. The initial decision upheld the rule in its entirety; however on Nov. 14, 2000 the appellate court ruled to delete section 37.199 of the rule. This deleted section required monetary compensation for the denial of accessible services. On March 8, 2001 the DOT amended the final ADA OTR bus rule to reflect this change. It should be noted that this change does not affect ADA accessibility requirements for OTR buses, nor does it prevent people from seeking judicial remedies under the ADA.

The Rule—So, what does the final rule say? Well for starters, beginning in October 2000 large fixed route OTR bus companies must provide service in an accessible bus upon 48 hours advance notice. As soon as the final rule was released Greyhound held a press conference and announced that it would make all 4,000 stops on its nationwide bus system accessible to wheelchair-users by Oct. 1999, one full year ahead of the official deadline. Of course this didn't come to pass, and it wasn't until April 2000 that passengers could actually book space in advance on an accessible bus.

Today, passengers that require accessible services should call Greyhound's ADA Assist Line at (800) 752-4841, at least 48 hours prior to their departure. If you're not able to make advance arrangements, Greyhound claims they will still make every reasonable effort to accommodate passengers, without delaying their bus departure schedules. In other words, they will do what they can if you just show up, so it's best to make advance arrangements, especially around holidays and peak travel periods.

Under the new rule, it's also considered discrimination for any OTR bus company to deny transportation to a person with a disability, or to require a passenger to reschedule their trip in order to receive accessible transportation. Greyhound does not prohibit passengers with disabilities from traveling alone, unless they require assistance with personal services. Greyhound provides personal care assistants (PCAs) with free passage, when they travel with a person with a disability. A free one way ticket is issued to the PCA at the time of travel. If the PCA requires a round trip ticket, another one-way ticket must be picked up at the time of the return trip.

Unfortunately the new rule stopped short of requiring accessible lavatories on board OTR buses. This fact was further emphasized by Sherman Qualls, Greyhound's Director of ADA Compliance. Sherman was a speaker at a travel conference I attended, and he proceeded to drone on about how Greyhound has gone out of their way to make their services accessible, because it's just "the right thing to do". Sherman talked about how Greyhound "goes the distance to make travel a pleasant and convenient experience for passengers with disabilities". He explained that Greyhound provided all of these services for people with disabilities out of the kindness of their corporate heart. In short they wanted to serve this market.

I looked around at the crowd, which appeared to falling for this fairy tale, hook, line and sinker. Then, there was a question from the back of the room, "Does Greyhound have accessible bathrooms on their buses?" asked a travel agent. The answer was a curt, "No, we're not required to do that under the ADA." Sherman then went on to berate the unfairness of ADA, and to explain how much this regulatory legislation was costing Greyhound. So much for "serving the market" and "doing the right thing!"

In any case, even though OTR bus companies are not required to provide accessible on board lavatories, the new rule does require them to provide boarding assistance to passengers with disabilities at rest stops. Adequate time must also be allocated for these passengers to use the restroom facilities. This rule applies at all stops which are least 15 minutes long; so, if you need to use the facilities at a rest stop, be sure to inform the driver.

The new rule allows passengers to travel safely in their own wheelchairs; however you still need to be aware of the liability limitations for damage to assistive devices. Greyhound's liability for damage to anything carried in the baggage compartment is only $250 per item. This includes wheelchairs and other assistive devices. This pittance won't go very far if there is any substantial damage to your assistive device, so be sure you have adequate insurance coverage. Check your existing insurance policies first to see if you are covered, then ask your agent about low cost options for additional coverage. In the long run, it's better to be safe than sorry.

One of the best provisions in the new rule for OTR buses addresses the future. The new rule requires OTR bus companies to install lifts on 50% of their fleets by 2006, and on 100% of their fleets by 2012. According to Sherman Qualls, in 2000 Greyhound already had 95 lift-equipped buses in their fleet. Each lift equipped bus has two tie-down positions for passengers who wish to remain in their own wheelchairs. Sherman also assured me that more accessible buses are on order. Personally I look forward to the future, and hope that Greyhound will indeed be able to abide by the final rule.

Personal Stories—Of course nothing speaks out better than personal experience, so here are a few anecdotes from real life Greyhound travelers. Is Greyhound living up to their end of the accessibility deal? You be the judge.

From Pennsylvania: I had a wonderful ride on a Greyhound Bus from Harrisburg to Pittsburgh on May 19, 2000. Making the reservation was not a smooth process, and it left me with great doubt as to whether or not I would actually get a bus with a lift. To add a margin of safety, I made a special trip down to the bus station to physically buy a ticket the night before. The next day I was pleasantly surprised, as my bus actually had a lift! There were two wheelchair sites, side by side. It took a small army of about 10 bus employees to figure out how to use the lift and tie down my wheelchair properly. Due to the space required for my wheelchair, six regular seats were folded or were otherwise unusable. However, those seats were still sold, so the passengers had to sit or stand in the aisle. But the driver was jolly and so were the passengers, and in the end I had a gorgeous ride through the heart of Pennsylvania.

From Texas: We were scheduled to leave Dallas, Texas at 11:00 PM on September 26,1999. I checked in with the station master, who told me the bus was late. She also said an employee would help me board the bus when it arrived. We went outside and waited by the double doors for the bus. The bus pulled in, and the large African-American driver approached me. I told him I was an ADA passenger and would need some assistance boarding the bus. His reply was "Cracker, the line is over there and you are not getting on my bus." I immediately reported this to the station master. She instructed another employee to go and help me board the bus. The driver saw us coming, and got back in his bus and drove off. He still had the baggage doors open, and some of the passengers were chasing the half-full bus. Needless to say, I didn't get on that bus!

From Washington: I took the Dirty Dog from Seattle to Portland on July 2, 2000. I notified the ADA line almost 72 hours before departure, and received confirmation the following day. I got to the terminal ½ hour before departure and the accessible bus wasn't there. The terminal manager came out and said he had my trip on the board, but it had somehow been ignored by the mechanics. He sent the driver back to pick up another bus, so we left Seattle about 25 minutes late. I couldn't believe I actually rode on Greyhound and (at long last) I wasn't treated like carry-on baggage.

Charter And Tour Companies—Technically the final rule applies to more than just Greyhound buses; and the rule will dramatically reshape the travel industry. Indeed the rule will make US travel more accessible, even if you never step foot on a Greyhound bus. Why? Well, because the rule also addresses charter bus services and tours. Beginning in October 2001 (for large companies) and in October 2002 (for small companies), charter and tour companies must provide service in an accessible vehicle upon 48 hours advance notice. This rule also applies to any other private demand-responsive transit service provider.

This does not mean that all the small charter and tour companies must purchase accessible buses; however, they must be able to provide them on 48 hours notice. The rule states that companies can do this by renting or leasing accessible vehicles. Additionally, disabled passengers cannot be charged extra, even if the charter company has to spend more money to provide accessible vehicles. The cost can however be passed on to all passengers in the form of higher prices. The accessible vehicle does not have to be a bus, and many charter companies may opt to rent a lift equipped van for this purpose. The choice is up to them, as long as they provide accessible transportation. Remember, "accessible" in this case, means lift or ramp equipped. Hand-carrying passengers on board is not considered appropriate under any circumstances.

Once all these regulations are in effect, more charter tours will be accessible. For example if you want to take the bargain gambling bus tour to Reno or Tahoe, all you will have to do is give the charter company 48 hours notice. Additionally package tours within the US will be more accessible, as tour operators will be required to provide accessible bus transportation on charter tours. This means that ultimately people with mobility disabilities will have more choices, as currently they are limited to booking tours with specialty tour operators that provide accessible tours. In the years to come more mainstream tour operators will be required to provide accessible tours, which means there will be more choices.

In the long run, this rule will make tours more accessible. In the short run, people with disabilities will most likely have to become skilled at self advocacy in order to get these services. So the most effective plan of action is to learn the rule, and then speak up for your rights.

6 | All Aboard

Train Travel

Train travel is much more than just a mode of transportation. Throughout time, "riding the rails" has been portrayed as an exciting and romantic way to travel. Whether you choose the Orient Express or the Northeast Express, there are many advantages to train travel. It's a great way to enjoy the countryside in relative comfort, and if you travel on a rail pass it's also very economical. As with everything else, train accessibility varies throughout the world. With that in mind, let's take a look at some of the major rail systems throughout the world, and see how they stack up access-wise.

Amtrak, USA—Amtrak, the US passenger rail carrier, operates routes throughout the country and even (a few) up into portions of Canada. Access varies, depending on the route and the train, but all Amtrak trains have at least one accessible coach car. Amtrak passengers can either travel in their own wheelchair or opt to transfer to a coach seat. All trains have wheelchair spaces, however there are no lock-downs on intercity trains. Some cars only have one wheelchair space, and no cars have more than two wheelchair spaces. Inquire about the specifics when you make your reservation. Power wheelchairs (if not in use) can be carried as checked baggage and manual wheelchairs can either be stowed in the passenger car, or carried as checked baggage. Amtrak can accommodate scooters and wheelchairs up to 30 inches wide by 48 inches long, and with a maximum passenger-occupied weigh of up to 600 pounds.

All wheelchair spaces, seats and even some "special" cars are for the exclusive use of people with disabilities (and their travel companions). In reality, Amtrak employees selectively enforce this priority seating policy. I've seen conductors tell able-bodied passengers they had to move because the seats were reserved for people with disabilities; however I've also seen employees treat wheelchair spaces as overflow luggage storage compartments. Again, it depends on the employee, the train and the route.

Many trains have accessible bathrooms, but the configuration varies depending on the train. Make sure and inquire about bathroom accessibility when you make your reservation. Don't be afraid to ask for the dimensions and measurements of the onboard bathroom, as there is no standard. Most onboard bathrooms are smaller than their "land versions", so don't expect to find features like a 5 foot turn around radius in the stall. Still, they are accessible to a large majority of the population, but it's always a best to ask for measurements in advance, so you won't encounter any unexpected surprises.

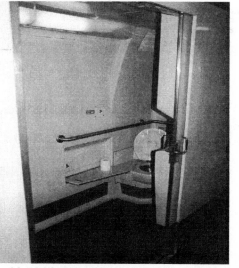

"Accessible" bathroom on Amtrak's Northeast direct train.

Amtrak offers two types of accessible sleeping accommodations; the Superliner and the Viewliner accessible bedrooms. The Superliner accessible bedroom has two berths, an accessible bathroom and takes up the entire width of the car. The Viewliner accessible bedroom can accommodate three passengers, but it's most comfortable for two passengers. It features two berths, a sofa and an accessible bathroom. There is one accessible bedroom in each sleeping car, and the availability and type depends on the route. Advance reservations are a must, as these accessible bedrooms go fast. Under a 1998 Department of Justice (DOJ) settlement, Amtrak must only allow passengers with a mobility disability to reserve an accessible bedroom up until 14 days prior to the departure date from the train's city of origin.

Amtrak employees will assist you in a variety of ways during your journey. Meal service is available to all passengers with disabilities. You may order from the menu and have the attendant deliver your food to your seat or bedroom. On some long distance routes wheelchair-users may transfer to and from the lounge cars at appropriate stops. Assistance with these transfers is available upon request. Amtrak employees will also assist you with reasonable food preparation tasks, such as opening packages and cutting meat. Additionally, on-board staff will help you board and leave the train and assist you in reaching the accessible bathroom.

Of course, boarding options vary depending on the train and the station, but all Amtrak stations offer at least one accessible boarding option. Some stations have raised platforms, and wheelchair-users can roll right on to the train. Be careful at stations with raised platforms, as many times there is a substantial gap between the train and the platform. Many stations have bridge plates that can be put down to eliminate this problem, so make sure and ask an employee about this option. Not all stations have raised platforms, and there are many boarding options for these stations. Some trains have on-board wheelchair ramps or wheelchair lifts, and most stations also have manual lifts. So, even if there is a mechanical failure of the on-board lift, the manual lift at the station can be used in an emergency. At some stations, manual lifts are the only option for boarding wheelchair-users.

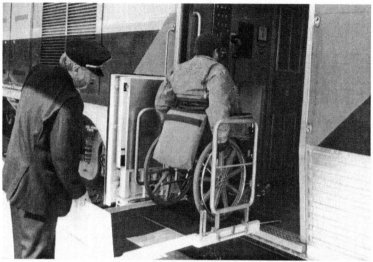

On-board lift on Amtrak's Capitol Corridor train.

Passengers may carry therapeutic oxygen on Amtrak trains, however there are a few restrictions. Oxygen tanks and associated equipment must not exceed 75 pounds per tank for a two tank system, or 20 pounds per tank for a six tank system. One passenger can carry a maximum of two 75 pound tanks or six 20 pound tanks. If your oxygen equipment requires the use of on-board power, you must carry at least a 12 hour backup supply of oxygen that does not require the use of on-board power. You may have to carry more than one battery in order to meet this requirement. All oxygen tanks must be secured while on board, and any wheels fastened to oxygen tanks must be removed for the duration of the trip. You must notify the reservation agent that you will be carrying therapeutic oxygen, so that the appropriate arrangements can be made. It's recommended that you estimate your total travel time, and then carry 20% more oxygen to make sure that you have an adequate supply. For safety reasons, oxygen tanks are not permitted in any cars that have a smoking area, however you can keep them in the enclosed area of a private sleeping room. In this case, you must keep the door closed and refrain from smoking for the duration of the trip.

Under a 1998 DOJ settlement, Amtrack implemented a number of discounts for passengers with mobility disabilities. All passengers with disabilities get a 15% discount off the published fare. Additionally an adult companion (16 years or older) may accompany a passenger with a mobility disability at 15% off the published fare. Passengers with mobility disabilities also get 30% off the published fares for accessible bedrooms. To obtain these discounted fares, call 800-USA-RAIL and mention the discounts available for passengers with mobility disabilities.

Another DOJ settlement addresses the Amtrak Thruway buses used in California. On several California Amtrak routes, transportation is provided by a combination of bus and rail service. Most of the Thruway buses are accessible but because of this September 2000 settlement, access will improve. All Thruway buses are now required to install improved securement and restraint features. These access upgrades will take place over the next three years. Thruway bus operators will also be expanding and standardizing the training provided to drivers and maintenance personnel to help ensure that access features remain in working order.

Amtrak publishes an *Access Amtrak* print guide for passengers with disabilities. Call 800-USA-RAIL or 877-268-7252 to receive your free copy. Alternative formats of this print guide are available in Braille, large print, audio tape and on diskette. Amtrak also posts updated access information on their website at *www.amtrak.com*.

VIA Rail, Canada—With the exception of a few Amtrak routes, rail service in Canada is operated by VIA Rail, the Canadian national rail carrier. Most VIA Rail trains are wheelchair accessible, except for some trains running between London and Sarina, Ontario. Accessibility varies throughout the system and is dependent on the specific route and equipment.

The most accessible VIA Rail passenger coaches are the LRC VIA 1 first class coaches. Each first class coach has wheelchair tie-downs and an accessible bathroom. The accessible bathroom has grab bars and a sliding door with an entry width of 35 inches. Some standard coach cars also come equipped with tie-downs and an accessible bathroom. The major difference in these two types of coach cars is the door width between the cars. On the first class cars the width is 28 inches, while on the standard coach cars it is only 25 inches. These VIA Rail coaches also come equipped with reduce-a width tools, which are used to help manual wheelchairs fit through the smaller doorways.

Most VIA Rail stations do not have raised boarding platforms, so wheelchair-users are boarded either with the use of a station lift or with the help of VIA Rail personnel. On some routes, passengers must provide their own boarding assistance. Contact VIA Rail in advance to find out if boarding assistance is available on a particular route.

VIA Rail uses a Washington Chair to board wheelchair-users who cannot stay in their own wheelchairs. This narrow chair has no arms and small wheels and is very similar to the aisle chairs used on airplanes. Wheelers are transferred to the Washington Chair for boarding, and then transferred to their seat. Once on board the train, wheelchair-users must use the Washington Chair to move about the train or to use the bathroom. VIA Rail personnel are available to assist passengers with the Washington Chair en route.

Folding manual wheelchairs can be stored in the coach cars. VIA Rail also accepts wheelchairs as checked baggage, as long as the owner travels by rail in at least one direction. In most cases, power wheelchairs cannot exceed 150 pounds, or be wider than 32 inches, or be longer or higher than 72 inches. In some cases VIA Rail will accept power wheelchairs as baggage if the total weight does not exceed 250 pounds. This applies only as long as the origination and destination stations have the proper facilities to load and unload them. Check with VIA Rail in advance for specifics on station equipment.

On transcontinental trains, passengers who cannot access the dining car or snack counters may have their meals served in their compartment. Make sure and inform a VIA Rail employee if you require this service. Some VIA Rail sleeping cars can also accommodate stretchers. A minimum of 48 hours advance notice is required for stretcher travel. Passengers who use therapeutic oxygen are allowed to bring their own equipment aboard, but they must give VIA Rail 48 hours advance notice. VIA Rail can provide voltage regulators on certain trains, but passengers are required to provide adequate battery backup for their equipment.

Advance arrangements (usually 48 hours) are required for accessible services on VIA Rail. Passengers must be able to attend to their own personal needs for the duration of the trip. VIA Rail employees are not required to assist passengers with eating, medical or personal hygiene tasks. Passengers who cannot attend to their own personal care must be accompanied by an escort. VIA Rail provides free economy class passage to required escorts.

For more information on VIA Rail service, call 888-842-7245 in the United States, or 800-561-8630 in Canada. Visit VIA Rail on the internet at *www.viarail.ca*.

BritRail, United Kingdom—BritRail, the national rail network of the United Kingdom, is made up of over two dozen regional rail carriers. These regional carriers provide rail service to Scotland, Wales, and England. To compliment this regional service, high-speed Eurostar trains travel under the English Channel to connect the United Kingdom with continental Europe. Under the provisions of the Disability Discrimination Act of 1995, all of these regional rail companies are required to provide service to passengers with disabilities. Of course, access varies from do-able to excellent, depending on the route you choose.

The first step in planning a BritRail trip is to determine where your journey will begin. Although this sounds like simplistic advice, it's really quite useful as the rail company that services your departure station is responsible for access arrangements throughout your entire rail journey. This applies even if you travel on several other regional rail companies throughout your trip. From the US, contact BritRail (877-677-1066) to find out what regional rail company services your departure station. If you're within Britain, contact National Rail Enquiries (0845 7 48 49 50) to obtain this information. Ask for the phone number of the local rail company, and contact them directly to make the arrangements for your entire rail journey.

According to BritRail public relations department, you can make arrangements directly with BritRail, however in practice this method doesn't really work. My friend Carol tried this method while she was planning her recent trip to Britain. Carol says of her experience, "When I called BritRail here in the US, none of the agents could answer my questions regarding access, or make the appropriate arrangements for me. In fact they hadn't the foggiest idea of what to do with me, or even where to begin. Unfortunately I got similar results on all my inquires directly to BritRail. I got the best results when I dealt directly with the regional rail companies."

In truth, BritRail's primary function is to sell rail passes to overseas travelers. These rail passes are good for unlimited train travel over a specific period of time, and they can be a great bargain if you plan to do a lot of train travel. So, plan your route, check out the access, and then calculate your fares. If a rail pass proves to be bargain then buy it directly from BritRail before you leave home; but don't rely on BritRail for access information, as you will literally be left waiting at the station.

Although access varies from one regional rail company to the next, there are some general guidelines that hold true throughout the system. Generally you will find the best access in the manned stations in the larger cities. Access to the rural stations varies widely, and in some cases wheelchair-users even have to be carried up steps. Accessible ground transportation is also more difficult to find in the smaller rural stations. Remember to ask a lot of questions regarding station access when you make your reservations. The best method is to ask the employee to describe the station access, rather than just asking if it is accessible. Even if they say the station is accessible, it's always good to follow up with, "How many steps are there?" You'll be surprised at how many times the answer will be, "Only two."

The maximum width for wheelchairs is 26.5" and the maximum length is 47", and none of the regional rail companies will "officially" carry scooters. However, says Carol of her recent BritRail trip, "Nothing was ever said to me about my scooter, and my feeling is that scooter users should be OK if your scooter measures less than the maximum allowable wheelchair. You must be able to maneuver in tight quarters. If you primarily use your scooter for distance, don't try it, as accessing many of the wheelchair spots requires some tight turns."

You should confirm your reservation and access arrangements at least 24 hours in advance, and even further ahead in peak travel seasons. And always allow plenty of time for connections.

Eurostar service to continental Europe is a great deal, as wheelchair-users get to ride in first class while paying coach fares. There are two designated seating areas for wheelchair users in first class coaches 9 and 10. Wheelchair-users are allowed to stay in their own chairs in these seating areas. Accessible toilets are also located in coaches 9 and 10. It's a great way to travel, as you can be in Paris in just under three hours. Says my friend Mark of his Eurostar Experience, "It was a smashing three hour trip, and even though I didn't get the free meal, I could access the toilet. It's a great deal for wheelers."

For more information about accessible services on Eurostar trains, call +44 1233 617575 or visit *www.eurostar.co.uk*.

Although not entirely rail-related, the *Smooth Ride Guide to the United Kingdom* is an excellent resource . In addition to contact information for the various regional rail companies, this handy guide contains detailed accessibility information on hotels and attractions throughout the United Kingdom. It's available for $16 (plus $9 shipping and handling) from Smooth Ride Guides, 01279-777966, fax: 01279-777995. I highly recommend it!

Europe, Eurail—European rail travel has long been touted as a very economical way to see Europe. Economy aside, it can also be a very accessible. I do stress "can-be", as advance planning is essential. You will however, be well rewarded for your research efforts, because with proper planning you can choose the most accessible Eurail routes, and avoid taking those not-so-accessible trans-European commuter flights. Additionally, you can save money by purchasing a Eurail pass before you leave home.

Like BritRail, the Eurail network is made up of many regional carriers. These regional carriers are usually country-specific, but some long distance trains do cross over borders. Also included in the Eurail network are some regional ferry and bus routes that connect the train network. So, when planning your Eurail vacation, make certain you investigate access on all modes of transportation along your route.

As you can imagine, access varies throughout Europe; however, regional carriers in Finland, France, Germany, Italy, Netherlands, Spain, Sweden and Switzerland "officially" offer some type of access. Even in those countries the access varies depending on the route. Remember, your rail travels don't have to necessarily be limited to those countries, as some long distance trains do cross over borders.

The best bet is to contact the regional carrier directly. Although there are several outlets that sell rail passes in the United States, these offices have very little knowledge of the true accessibility of the trains. You need to contact the regional carrier directly to find out the access details. For example, even though it is possible to travel by rail in Italy, power wheelchairs can only be carried in baggage cars. So although most rail pass outlets can tell you that Italy trains do provide "disabled access", most are unaware of specific details such as this. Contact the rail pass offices for information on rail passes, and contact the regional carriers for access information.

Rail passes are very economical, but please note that there are many different types. Most passes are valid for unlimited travel within a certain time frame. Some passes cover only one country, some cover a combination of countries and some cover the entire network. Plan your route before you purchase a rail pass, as the economical value of a rail pass is directly dependent on your needs.

Even though not all trains are officially accessible, some are do-able. It really depends on your ability and attitude. My friend Jack spent several weeks riding the rails in Europe last year. Jack is in his mid twenties, loves to travel, and is in pretty good physical shape. He traveled throughout Europe with a friend. Although he had a great time, he readily admits there were a few "incidents". Here's his recollection of one of the more memorable glitches of his trip. "I had a great time in Europe, although some of the trains I took didn't exactly have roll-on access. At several stations, Tim had to pick me up and carry me on the train, and then go back and get my wheelchair. This worked OK, except for one time when the train left the station before Tim had a chance to load my wheelchair. At the time, I was hysterical. We both just kept shouting 'rollstuhl', which is the German word for wheelchair. I thought I'd never see my Quickie again. It all worked out OK, and eventually I was reunited with my wheelchair, but it was a very stressful situation."

But don't let Jack's rollstuhl experience dissuade you from train travel in Europe. Some trains have excellent facilities. For example the French rail carrier SNCF has wheelchair spaces on all TGV and Corail trains. These spaces are located in first class compartments, but wheelchair-users who purchase second class tickets are able to reserve them at no extra charge. It works much like the system on the Eurostar trains. Advance reservations are a must for this and many other access arrangements. Contact the regional carriers for specific information.

Most rail pass offices should be able to give you contact information for the regional rail carriers. You can also search the internet under "Eurail" for general information on the Eurail network and rail pass retailers. The European Commission also puts out some great access guides which include some information about train travel. These free country-specific guides are only available on-line in PDF format at europa.eu.int/comm/dg23/tourism/tourism-publications/travel_guides.html.

Australia, Rail Australia—Rail Australia provides support to the international market for the major tourist orientated passenger rail operators in Australia. These include Queensland Rail which operates passenger rail service in Queensland, Countrylink which is based in New South Wales, and the Great Southern Railway which is based in South Australia and includes the worlds famous Indian Pacific route.

Access varies depending on the route. Not all trains have wheelchair spaces, so wheelchair-users may have to use a boarding chair and then transfer to their seat. The best station access is generally found at the larger city terminals, however even the Alice Springs station now has a lift.

The XP trains operated by Countrylink are nicely accessible. The XP trains operate on the Sydney to Brisbane, Sydney to Melbourne and Sydney to Dubbo routes. One car per train has a wheelchair space, lock-down straps and an accessible toilet. These features allow wheelchair-users to remain in their own wheelchairs for the duration of the trip.

Another route with nicely accessible facilities is the Indian Pacific trans-continental train. The Indian Pacific is one of the worlds longest train routes (4352 km), and connects Sydney and Perth. The Indian Pacific train features a specially designed "access cabin" which has ample room to maneuver and an accessible toilet and shower. The access cabin sleeps two, and has an upper and lower bunk. It's a great way to see the varied landscape of Australia, as the train travels from the Blue Mountains to the Nullarbor Plains.

A variety of money-saving rail passes are also available through Rail Australia. Contact Rail Australia for specific access information, or for contact information for regional rail providers. Rail Australia can be reached at +61-8-8217-4681 or fax +61-8-8217-4682 . Visit their website at _www.railaustralia.com.au_.

7 | Finding The Right Room

If I've heard it once, I've heard it a thousand times, "I reserved an accessible room and when I got there I couldn't even get into the bathroom." Of course there are many variations on that theme, but it all boils down to the same issue; appropriate access. What is appropriate access? Well, that varies from person to person, because what's adequate for one person may not necessarily meet the needs of another person. That's what makes finding the right hotel room such a challenge; as not only are people's needs different, but so are access standards.

What Is Accessible?—How can you tell if a property has accessible rooms? Well, the first thing you have to do is define "accessible". That's a tall order; and in fact the experts have been trying to do it for years. The truth is, there's no one uniform definition of "accessible". Many properties have developed their "own" access criteria, but even these standards vary widely from property to property. It's definitely not what you would call uniform. It would be great if an accessible room at Hotel X in St. Paul was exactly the same as an accessible room at Hotel Y in Amarillo, but that's just not the way it works. Even that "little blue wheelchair pictogram" can have many meanings, depending on how and where it's displayed.

For example, in California (where I live) if you see that blue wheelchair pictogram posted at the entrance to a hotel, it means that the entrance to that hotel is accessible. It doesn't necessarily mean that anything else within that property is accessible. It may or may not be; but basically it's a crap shoot. The same pictogram is often prominently featured in advertisements for hotels and motels. What does it mean? Well, that depends on the property. Generally speaking, there's no uniform criteria or any standardized usage of the international accessibility pictogram. In fact, two properties right next door to one another may have different accessibility criteria; yet, both may also proudly display that little blue wheelchair pictogram. But, you may ask, "how can this be possible in the United States, where we have access laws such as the Americans with Disabilities Act (ADA)?" To answer that question, you need to understand a few things about the ADA, so let's take a brief look at how it addresses accessibility in the lodging industry.

Properties constructed after Jan. 26, 1992 are subject to the new construction guidelines of the ADA. Under this criteria, new properties are required to have a minimum number of accessible rooms, which ranges from 2% to 4% of the number of total rooms, depending on the size of the property. This criteria also specifically defines access features required in the accessible rooms; however inclusion of some of these access features is also dependent upon the size of the property. For example, if a property has 50 or more rooms, it must have a minimum number of rooms with roll-in showers. Again, this depends on the total number of rooms, and it ranges between 2% to 4% of the number of total rooms. Properties with less that 50 rooms are not required to have any rooms with roll-in showers, however they still must have a minimum number of accessible guest rooms. So, an accessible guest room, does not always have a roll-in shower. This only applies to new construction, not to remodeled properties.

Properties constructed before Jan. 26, 1992 are subject to different guidelines under the ADA. The ADA states that these existing facilities are required to remove architectural barriers where "readily achievable". "Readily achievable" is defined as "being easy to accomplish, and able to be carried out without much difficulty or expense". So, as you can see, the definition of "readily achievable" is open to interpretation, as "cost" and "difficulty" are sometimes relative terms. In fact, what might be readily achievable for a large hotel chain would not necessarily be readily achievable for a small owner-operated motel. So, two properties next door to one another could in fact have "ADA compliant rooms" with completely different access features. It's pretty easy to do, especially when you talk about "readily achievable".

Additionally, some cities and states have local access codes; and where two laws conflict, the more stringent of the two applies. Sometimes it's the ADA, sometimes it is not. And then you have "historical" buildings, which may or may not be subject to access standards. Indeed, sometimes it takes an attorney to decide exactly how the ADA applies to public entities.

If you take only one thing away from this chapter, remember this; never just ask for an accessible room, because there isn't a universal standard for accessible rooms, even within the United States. The term "accessible" or "ADA compliant" is meaningless, unless you understand how the property defines it; and to do that you have to learn to ask a lot of questions.

Ask The Right Questions—In order to get accurate answers to your questions, you need to ask the right people. Always call the property directly, rather than calling the central reservation number. Sometimes access improvements at a local property are not entered in the central reservation database. Reservation agents at the property are usually able to give you more updated and detailed access information. They are more familiar with the property. In fact, many properties include a tour of the rooms and public areas, as part of their reservation agent training program.

We've already determined that you should never just call up a property, ask for an accessible room, book it and then hang up. Many reservation clerks assume that their "accessible rooms" are the one-size-fits-all solution for every traveler. The results are disastrous, and many novice travelers end up in "ADA compliant" rooms that don't meet their needs. Most likely your conversation will go something like this. After you say you need an accessible room, the reservation agent will tell you that they have "ADA compliant rooms". "Great", you reply. Your next step is to ask the reservation agent to describe the "ADA compliant room".

Ask the reservation agent to describe the access features of the room. Try to refrain from asking the reservation agent yes or no questions. For example, instead of asking if there is a roll-in shower in the bathroom, ask the agent to describe the bathroom. Additionally, be especially careful about asking yes or no questions in the Orient, as many customer service employees consider it rude to answer a question (any question) with a "no". If there is a particular access feature that is important to you (such as an open frame bed), make sure you specifically inquire about that feature. Never assume anything.

Of course, even when you call the property directly, you can still be in for some surprises. I remember one time I called a hotel and asked if they had any accessible rooms with roll-in showers. Not a hard question, right? Well, apparently the reservation agent was new, or just didn't understand the question or was having a really bad day. After talking with me for about 10 minutes she put me on hold and vowed to find an answer to my perplexing question. After about five minutes she came back on the line and breathlessly replied, "We have kits that we can put in the shower so that deaf people can use the shower." Then she shouted, "Are you deaf?"

Which brings me to my next point. Trust your instincts. If you think you are talking with a flake, hang up and start over. There is a high turnover rate with reservation agents. The good ones go on to better jobs and the bad ones either get fired or keep at it. So, if the reservation agent makes no sense at all, or if you get bad vibes, or if you think they don't understand what you are asking; don't take any chances. You're probably right in your assessment of the situation. Just say, thank you, hang up and start over; either with that property or with your next pick.

If for some reason, the reservation clerk seems competent, but is just having problems describing the room, ask if they have ever been in the room. If the reply is "no," then ask to speak to somebody who has been in the room. If the reservation agent doesn't seem to know who to talk with, ask to speak to somebody in housekeeping. Nobody knows the rooms better than the housekeeping staff, as they have to clean them each and every day.

Don't be afraid to ask for specific measurements. If door width is a concern, ask for that measurement. Don't forget about the door width of the interior (bathroom) doors too. Dennis Ciesielski of Menomonie, WI came up with a good procedure for finding out the specifics about important measurements. After inquiring about the details of an accessible room, he then asks the clerk to fax him a floorplan (with measurements) of the room. How's it working? So far, Dennis reports that all of his requests have been fulfilled. He also adds, "Perhaps if people asked for floorplans more often, properties would have this information readily available." So, when in doubt about measurements, ask the reservation agent to fax you a floor plan of the accessible room.

Sometimes you need to employ a little creativity when making your lodging arrangements. For example, if you need some specific equipment in your room, and the reservation agent doesn't seem to understand the difference between a shower chair and a pool chair, then try this little technique. When the conversation reaches an impasse, try communicating your needs with a photograph. Snap a photo of your assistive device and fax it to the property. If you don't have a camera, then a good source for photographs is "A Resource Guide for Hotels & Motels". This handy guide contains descriptions and photographs of a wide variety of assistive devices. You can copy the pages and fax them to hotels, or take it to your travel agent to illustrate your needs. It's also a great resource for travel agents. "A Resource Guide for

Hotels & Motels" is available for $10, from CAT/UB Products (800-628-2281). Remember, a picture is worth a thousand words. Indeed, some travelers come up with very unique options for procuring special equipment while on the road. Says frequent-traveler Ann, "I need to sleep with my head elevated, but I've often found it difficult and expensive to get a hospital bed delivered to my hotel room. My solution is to contact a furniture rental company and rent a recliner. It's usually a lot cheaper (and easier) than renting a hospital bed. However, I always remember to first ask the hotel if they have a recliner they can put in my room. Sometimes they do, and then I get it for free. Of course this won't work for everybody, but I'm very comfortable sleeping in a recliner."

Finally, always request a written confirmation notice that includes the specifics of your reserved accessible room. Bring this confirmation notice with you when you check into the hotel. Additionally, I always ask for the name of the reservation agent; in fact I even ask them to spell it, for emphasis. Sometimes when people know you have their name, they tend to do a better job, as they are more accountable. It's not a 100% guarantee, but it takes so little time, and the benefits far outweigh the effort.

Block That Room—Have you ever arrived at a hotel, reservation in hand, only to discover that your accessible room had been given to another guest? Well, you're not alone. More and more travelers are learning that a reservation by itself doesn't necessarily guarantee an accessible room upon arrival. So, what's a traveler to do? Basically you need to learn how to separate the wheat from the chaff so you can become an effective self advocate. In order to do this, you need to get the inside scoop on some lodging industry practices.

First, you need to understand a little bit about hotel reservation systems. The ability to reserve an accessible room is directly dependent upon the type of reservation software used by a specific property. Generally speaking, the older reservation software doesn't give reservation agents the flexibility to reserve a specific room. In this case, a reservation for an "accessible room" is treated as a request, and it's entered as free text into the reservation system. In other words, a specific accessible room cannot be reserved. Fortunately many hotel chains have updated their reservation software in order to be Y2K compliant. Most of the newer reservation software allows properties to reserve a specific room; but only to the extent that the properties have defined their specific room types in the computer system. So, in most cases if a hotel has flagged their accessible rooms, the newer software can reserve a specific accessible room.

The only way to determine if a property can reserve an accessible room is to ask; however, be careful how you phrase your query. Many people ask if the property will "guarantee" the room. This is the wrong terminology, as in hotel-ese "guarantee" means "to secure with a credit card deposit." In other words, your reservation will be guaranteed with your credit card number. This locks in your rate, and assures you that a room will be there for you, even if you arrive late. It does not, however, insure that your room will be accessible. The correct way to phrase your request is, "Can you block that accessible room for me?" In hotel terminology, "block" means to reserve a specific room for a specific guest.

Of course, even if you ask the right questions, you may still go through a lot of properties before you get the appropriate responses. Basically it's a numbers game. You just have to keep calling until you find a property that doesn't hem and haw about blocking accessible rooms. The best way to speed up your search is to begin with properties that have a better than average chance of answering your query affirmatively. Here are a few places to start:

- Microtel CEO Mike Levin claims their company will block accessible rooms upon reservation. Although there is no written policy on this matter, in practice Microtel seems to follow through on Levin's promise.

- Motel 6 claims it will reserve and block accessible rooms. In practice, accessible rooms are blocked; however, some guests have complained that many of the older (pre 1992) properties lack appropriate access.
- Hampton Inns have been very proactive about blocking accessible rooms. This is not a system wide policy, so make sure and inquire directly with the specific property.
- Under the terms of a 1996 Department of Justice (DOJ) settlement, all Marriott Courtyard properties are required to block their accessible rooms.
- All BASS Properties (Holiday Inn, Crowne Plaza and Staybridge Suites) are required to block their accessible rooms under the terms of a 1998 DOJ settlement.

Unfortunately it takes extra time to locate properties that block accessible rooms. There just seems to be no way around that, but perhaps in the years to come, more properties will adopt this as a standard practice. Until then, shop around, and remember; even the most accessible room in the world is useless, unless it's actually available when you arrive.

No (Accessible) Room At The Inn—Of course, sometimes even when you do everything right; you can still run into problems. What do you do then? What do you do when you arrive at a property and find out they don't have the appropriate room for you, even though you have a confirmed reservation? There are many answers to that question.

First off, if the property doesn't have any accessible rooms left, they must find you appropriate lodging at another hotel. Sometimes this is acceptable and sometimes it is not. For example if you chose a hotel because of it's location you might also want to ask for a transportation allowance. If it's really a big inconvenience to you, ask for a voucher for free stay on a future visit. These are both reasonable requests. Do not however, ask the property to foot the bill for your entire vacation. This is not considered a reasonable request, and in most cases, management won't even address your problem if you ask for something they view as being totally unreasonable.

However, in most cases, the solution is open to discussion. In truth there is no one right procedure for getting the best resolution, as it all depends on your own personal style. To illustrate this point, let me tell you a true story, about how three people handled the same problem in three completely different ways. The players in this little drama are Carol, John and James. The scene was the check-in counter of an upscale business hotel on the first day of a disability conference. All three players held a confirmed reservation for a specific type of accessible room. They all arrived at different times, only to find that their confirmed room type was "not available". Here's how they each handled it.

Carol was the first to arrive. Her reservation was for an accessible smoking room with a tub and shower. The desk clerk explained to Carol that the only accessible rooms left were non-smoking rooms. This was not acceptable to Carol. She quoted the law, and calmly explained her needs, and patiently reasoned with the clerk. In the end, the clerk handed her an astray and told her to ignore the no smoking signs in the room. Problem solved. As a non-smoker I cringe when I consider the resolution, but as a disability rights advocate I applaud Carol's victory.

John was the next to arrive. He was accompanied by Phil, his PCA (personal care attendant). John's reservation was for an accessible room, with 2 beds and a roll-in shower. There were no accessible rooms with 2 beds available. Now John is a very astute businessman, with a no-nonsense approach to life. After reviewing the law with the clerk, John quipped that he had no intention of sleeping in the same bed with Phil. He added that he was very tired, and that if they didn't provide him with an appropriate room, he would sleep on the sofa in the lobby. Of course John added, "I sleep in the nude." Problem solved. In short order, the clerk found an appropriate room for John and Phil.

There were no accessible rooms left by the time James arrived. However this good looking, 20-something young man didn't let that stop him. He effortlessly explained the law, and slowly won over the clerk with his charm. His southern accent didn't hurt matters either. James ended up with the accessible penthouse suite.

So, who's the best problem-solver? In truth, there's no winner, as they all achieved equally appropriate results. So, what's the most effective advocacy style? It's the one that works best for you. The first step is to learn the rules, know the law and understand your rights. Then find your style, fine-tune it, and add it to your advocacy toolbox. It may take some time, and a bit of trial and error, so be flexible until you find a style that works for you. It's not an exact science, but it is effective. It's the way to get results.

B&Bs and Inns—Although many people overlook small Inns and Bed & Breakfasts (B&Bs) when searching for accessible lodgings, some of these owner-operated properties are in fact nicely accessible. Under the law, these smaller properties aren't required to be accessible if they're owner-occupied; however, many are, either because of need or design. For example if one of the owners or a family member is disabled, then it's quite likely that their property will be accessible. Additionally, many of these small property owners don't want to loose any wedding business, so they've made their properties accessible. They want to be able to accommodate all the friends and relatives of the wedding party. Smart business people don't want to have to turn business away, and indeed the B&B business is very competitive.

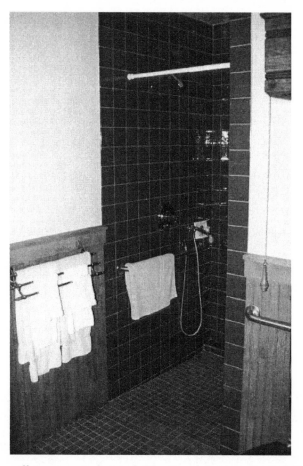

Many small inns are nicely accessible. Pictured here is the bathroom of
Mae's Room at the Redbud Inn in Murphys, CA.

Additionally, some designs just lend themselves better to
access than others. For example many older homes have nice
hardwood floors, and wide double doors. In short, it never hurts
to ask about access; but again, be sure to ask the clerk to describe the access features. One advantage to staying at a small
Inn or B&B is that the owners are very familiar with their rooms,
and most can describe them down to the smallest detail. Additionally, many smaller properties, including B&Bs and Inns have

the ability to reserve specific rooms. In fact, it's standard practice at many B&Bs to reserve a specific room for each guest. So, it you reserve an accessible room, you can rest assured that it will be available when you arrive.

A great source of access information on small Inns and B&Bs is the InnSeekers database. This free database is available 24 hours a day, by phone or on the internet. You can search for properties by location and by the level of access (some, or full wheelchair access). To access this handy database, call 1-888-Inn-Seek or visit *www.innseekers.com*.

Hostels—Hostels are another often overlooked accessible lodging option. Although hostelling first gained popularity in the 1970's as an inexpensive way for young people to see the world; today most hostels are open to travelers of all ages. The one exception is in Bavaria, Germany, were the age limit is 26.

Traditionally hostels provide inexpensive lodging in dormitory style bedrooms, with separate quarters for males and females. Today many hostels also have private family rooms which can be reserved in advance. Most hostels still have kitchens, and all have storage areas and public rooms. Some hostels even have swimming pools, barbecues and hot tubs. There really are a wide variety of hostel accommodations throughout the world. And, many hostels do have accessible facilities.

There are many advantages to hostelling. The major perk of course, is big savings on lodging costs, as nightly hostel rates run between $8-$17 per person. Rates vary depending on the location and the amenities of the property, so expect to pay more in the larger cities and less in the country. Another advantage to hostelling is that you can meet other travelers. And finally, cooking your meals can cut down on food costs. As far as access goes, most hostel proprietors are very familiar with the access features of their property. I've also found that they are incredibly honest about the access, as they don't want guests to be disappointed when they arrive.

Hostelling International (HI) maintains a worldwide database of hostels. Although membership is not required to stay in a HI hostel, members do get a discount. Members also receive a print copy of the HI hostel directory. The HI directory is also available on-line at *www.hiayh.org*. Accessible hostels are noted on the website, but access details are not listed. Contact the property directly to find out about specific access details. For more information about hostels, contact Hostelling International at 202-783-6161. And don't just limit yourself to hostels in the USA, as I've seem some wonderfully accessible hostels around the world.

Home Exchange—Home exchanging is not a new idea; in fact, it's been a popular practice in Europe for decades. Today the popularity of this money saving practice is moving across the Atlantic and catching on in North America. The good news is that home exchanging is the ideal solution for people who need accessible holiday accommodations. In fact, it kills two birds with one stone, as home exchanging is an accessible and affordable holiday option.

The principles behind home exchanging are pretty simple. The idea is to find somebody with a lifestyle similar to yours, in another part of the country or world. Then the two of you exchange homes; you both live in each others house while you are on holiday. It's an even exchange, so both exchangees pocket the money they would have spent on other lodging arrangements.

The benefits of home exchanging are obvious. If you have made some accessibility modifications to your own home, then it just makes sense to find another person like you, who has made similar modifications to their home. One of the best resources for accessible home exchange listings is the Vacation Home Swap Bulletin Board (*www.independentliving.org/vacex/index.html*). This internet resource is operated by the Institute on Independent Living in Stockholm, Sweden, and contains accessible home exchange listings from around the world. Visitors can browse through the listings, do a keyword search, or add their own home to the growing collection. There is no charge to view or post listings on this bulletin board.

There are a also a growing number of home exchange listing services. These vary by size and service, but most all of them charge a fee for their services. Some sell print directories, some offer internet access and some offer a combination of both services. Even though many of these listing services have a accessible home section, in reality most homes listed is those sections are not very accessible. Remember, people have different definitions of "accessible", and to some people an accessible home is one that has a wide front door. Truly the best source of accessible homes is the Vacation Home Swap Bulletin Board. Plus, it's also free!!

Many people feel funny about having a stranger live in their home. Indeed, caution should be used when screening a potential home exchange partner. In fact, many people turn to friends and relatives as home exchange partners. Some people post notices on school and work bulletin boards, and some people even meet exchange partners through friends. Truly there are no rules here, and you can be as creative as you want. Do what is most comfortable for you.

In any case, consider a home exchange for your next holiday. This tried and true European idea offers big monetary savings, plus the comfort and freedom of real accessibility.

8 | So You Want To Get Off The Ship?

Cruise Travel

Cruise travel has long been touted as the "most accessible vacation option" by a plethora of self-proclaimed travel industry experts. In reality, cruises are only an appropriate option for some people. Make no mistake about it, cruises are far from a barrier-free experience. It's true that some of the newer ships are very accessible; however the same can't be said of the older ships. Additionally, very few shore excursions offer roll-on access. In short, it takes a good amount of advance planning and preparation to insure adequate access on any cruise holiday.

So why does the travel industry continue to promote cruising as the most appropriate accessible travel choice? The answer to that is pretty simple; time and money. It takes a good deal of time and effort to package individual itineraries. Cruises already come in a nice neat package, so they are easy to sell. More importantly, in this day of dwindling commissions, cruise lines are still able to offer travel agents top dollar incentives for selling their product. In short, it just makes sense to promote a product that puts money in your pocket.

Now, don't let me discourage you from taking a cruise, if that's truly your heart's desire. I'm just trying to give you a realistic look at the situation, so you understand all of your options. Many inexperienced travel agents present cruise travel as the only option for accessible travel, and that's really a great disservice to the traveling public. If you truly want to take a land tour, then don't let a travel agent talk you into a cruise. Of course you should understand that some land tours present access barriers; but again, some cruises aren't that accessible either. It's truly a situation of buyer-beware. Don't assume all cruises are accessible. And if you are going to work with a travel agent, work with one who is well versed in accessible travel; not just in cruise travel.

Of course I know many people who've had glorious cruise experiences. These people either did a lot of advance planning themselves, or worked with a travel agent who was well versed in the intricacies of accessible travel. If you decide a cruise is for you, do keep a few things in mind. No matter how luxurious the rooms are or how decadent the food is; if you can't get off the ship it's just a long boat ride. Now some people can live with that; in fact some people just like the idea of getting on a ship and being pampered. However if you want more from your cruise experience, like being able to enjoy the ports, you have to jump in and do some research. Remember, access doesn't magically materialize just because you choose to cruise. Additionally, if you plan to visit foreign ports of call you need to become familiar with access in that country. Remember, when you are outside of the US you are not protected by the ADA; and truly in some places wheelchair-users are treated as second class citizens.

Access on the Seas—The Department of Justice (DOJ) has long held that cruise ships are covered under Title III of the Americans with Disabilities Act (ADA). According to John L. Wodatch, Chief of the DOJ Disability Rights Section, the ADA also applies to foreign flag cruise ships that dock at US ports, unless, as he says "there is a showing that the application of the ADA to a foreign flag cruise ship would conflict with an international convention to which the United States is a party." Seems pretty simple, right? Well not exactly. That point is aptly illustrated by Tammy Stevens much publicized experience with Premier Cruise Lines.

Tammy's saga began in 1998, when she saw an advertisement for a four-day cruise aboard Premier's *SS Oceanic*. The cruise was priced at an affordable $349, so she contacted her travel agent for more details. Her travel agent was assured by Premier that the *SS Oceanic* was indeed wheelchair accessible; however, a wheelchair accessible cabin was not available for the $349 price tag. Still, Tammy wanted to cruise, so she booked the trip, paid extra for her wheelchair accessible cabin, and looked forward to a relaxing cruise.

After the *SS Oceanic* set sail, Tammy discovered that her cabin was not wheelchair accessible. In order to use the bathroom, Tammy's sister and mother had to physically pick her up and put her on the commode, or set her in the shower. To say this was humiliating is a gross understatement. Tammy was also left with bruises all over her arms and legs from this procedure. To add insult to injury, Tammy further discovered that many of the ship's public areas were not wheelchair accessible. Such was the birth of Stevens v. Premier Cruises, Inc..

The US District Court ruled against Stevens on her original complaint. The judge found that Stevens didn't have the right standing (a legal technicality), and that the ADA does not apply to foreign flag cruise ships. Stevens request to amend her pleading was denied, so she appealed the decision. The appellate court ruled that Stevens should have had the opportunity to amend her original pleading. The appellate court also found that Title III of the ADA does apply to cruise ships, and the ADA does apply to foreign flag carriers.

So, where do we stand today in regards to the ADA and cruise ship access? The appellate court ruling actually established case law on the subject, which is an important first step in any ADA matter. The problem is that the US Access Board has not established any accessibility standards for passenger vessels (cruise ships). Look for that to change in the next few years though. The Passenger Vessel Access Advisory Committee submitted it recommendations to the Access Board on Dec. 18, 2000. The Access Board is now in the process of reviewing the recommendations, seeking public comments and refining the rules. Best guess is that the final rules will be completed by 2003, but that's only a guess. Sometimes the wheels of justice turn very slowly, especially in the rule making process.

So in theory, yes, cruise ships that call on US ports are covered under the ADA. However, since no accessibility standards currently exist, it's difficult to prevail in any ADA action involving cruise ship access. The ruling on the Stevens appeal does help strengthen the law, and hopefully it will also serve as an impetus for the rapid adoption of access standards for passenger vessels. For now, it's best to proceed with caution; and remember to ask about specific access details and features before booking any cruise. As evidenced in the Stevens case, "wheelchair accessible" can indeed have a very broad definition.

Service Animals—The DOJ rule regarding service animals is pretty explicit. It states that public accommodations must modify their policies, practices or procedures to accommodate service animals. And yes this includes cruise ships that dock in US ports. That's the short and easy part; the more difficult part is the documentation, preparation and (of course) the paperwork.

First things first; you can't just stroll on board a cruise ship with your service animal. You must inform the cruise line at the time you book your cruise that you will be traveling with a service animal. All cruise lines require a health certificate for service animals. You must present the health certificate at embarkation. Some cruise lines require additional forms. Some ports of call require even further documentation, and as mentioned in an earlier chapter, some countries impose quarantines on imported animals. If you dock at a country that has such a quarantine, your service animal will not be allowed off the ship. Make sure and find out about quarantines, restrictions and all required documentation in advance. This simple step will save you a lot of heartache.

What are your options if you can't take your service animal ashore? Basically you're limited to two options. You can stay on board while the ship is in port, or you can go ashore without your service animal. Of course the latter is only a realistic option if you are traveling with an able-bodied companion. Still it's something to consider if you really want to see the port.

Many cruise veterans also agree that it's a good idea to let the cruise line know about the size of your service animal in advance; just so there will be no surprises. Some people prefer to describe the animal (including the weight) while some people opt to send a photo of the animal.

One of the biggest concerns about service animals and cruises is the toileting arrangements (for the service animal that is). Is there really a poop deck? Well, there will be the week you cruise! Seriously, ask about the cruise line's toileting policy well in advance. It's also a good idea to get the policy in writing. Policies vary from cruise line to cruise line. Some cruise lines provide a wood box filled with mulch, while others provide Astroturf. It's a good idea to get your dog used to "non-grass" toileting prior to your cruise. In regards to that issue, I'm reminded of my friend Karen's predicament, when she took a cruise. Her service animal just wouldn't (or couldn't) do his business for days. Finally her husband took the dog out for a vigorous run around the deck, just to shake things up a bit. It worked like a charm; doggy did his business but hubby was pooped (no pun intended). The moral of the story is that it pays to familiarize you dog with toileting conditions similar to what you'll find on the ship.

It also pays to be prepared for the unexpected. Learn how to deal with problems when they arise. One cruise passenger who left his service animal in his cabin while he went ashore, found that his cabin steward refused to clean his cabin. Apparently the cabin steward was afraid of dogs. If you have an incident such as that, report it to the purser, remind him that it's an access issue, and request that appropriate accommodations be made. In the above case, an appropriate accommodation would have been to have another cabin steward clean the cabin.

Finally, a word of warning if you book a cruise and air package. Never rely on the cruise line to relay information about your service animal to the airline. Deal with the airline directly. For more information about air travel as it applies to service animals, see the *Up, Up And Away, Beyond Wheelchairs* chapter. Actually this tip applies to any disability related information. Never trust the cruise line to make access arrangements with the airline. Always contact the airline directly to confirm all access arrangements.

Cruise Lines—As with all tourism providers, some cruise lines just have a more proactive approach to access. Unfortunately there are also a few cruise lines at the other end of the spectrum too. There are several things you should take into consideration when choosing a cruse line, including the personality of the ships, the age of the fleet, and the type of passengers the line typically attracts. In the end it will be a decision based on your tastes and budget. However, be aware there are a few cruise lines that have a strange way of addressing (or not addressing) access issues. Here are a few examples.

Renaissance Cruise Lines tops my "bad boys" list, as they have actively chosen to ignore access issues. In fact, there is not one accessible cabin on any of their ships. This Fort Lauderdale based company features luxury cruises to exotic ports. They don't exactly sail small ships either; in fact over 75% of their ships can accommodate over 650 passengers each. You would think that there would be room for at least one accessible cabin on board each ship. But again, they have chosen to ignore this market. Renaissance Cruise Lines has a fairly new fleet. Over 60% of their fleet was built since 1999; so in theory it would have been easy to include some accessible cabins. Of course Renaissance does not call on any US ports, so it will most likely remain exempt for any access requirements implemented by the US Access Board. In short, don't even consider Renaissance Cruise Lines if you need any type of accessible accommodations.

There are also a few cruise lines that have some archaic attitudes about the disabled community. For example, Norwegian Cruise Lines requires that passengers with any type of a physical disability sign a "Mobility Impaired Passenger Release" form. This form advises passengers about possible access limitations of the ships, including 5-6 inch risers throughout the ships, bathroom door widths of 20-22 inches and inaccessible stairways. The form also states, "we request that you travel with an individual in your cabin who is not mobility impaired."

So what happens if you don't sign the form. Technically they have the right to refuse you passage. Is that legal under the ADA? In my opinion, it's discrimination to require a wheelchair-user to travel with an able-bodied companion, when the same restrictions are not imposed on able-bodied travelers. The airlines can't do that carte blanche, so why should the cruise lines be able to pull it off? So hopefully one day soon somebody will sue one of the cruise giants for disability-based discrimination. I'm sure that once a court precedent is set, the cruise lines will abolish their restrictive policies. For now, be aware that some cruise lines do require you to sign a release form, and if you don't abide by the rules, they can deny you passage. It's archaic at best. Why should people who live independently be required to travel with a companion? The bottom line is, they shouldn't. There are a lot of cruise lines to choose from, so don't do business with those that impose unreasonable restrictions on you. Remember, you do have a choice.

Additionally, don't assume that US cruise lines have the best access. In truth, access on US flag ships is evolving very slowly, and only because of pressure from within the disability community. Connie George, an old hand at booking cruises for people with disabilities, illustrates this point, as she relates her recent experience.

"In the spring of 2000 a deaf client inquired about a Hawaiian Island cruise for her upcoming honeymoon. I never use American Hawaii because they offer very poor physical access; however, since this client specifically wanted a Hawaiian Island cruise, American Hawaii was my only choice. I was shocked to learn that the parent company (which operates American Hawaii, United States Lines and Delta Queen) had some rather archaic views regarding people with disabilities."

"At the time of my inquiry, they required a hearing person to accompany a deaf passenger, a sighted person to accompany a blind passenger and a caregiver to accompany a wheelchair user. I couldn't believe what I heard, so I called back several times, and each time I was quoted the same policy by a different agent. I hit the roof. Something just had to be done about this discriminatory policy".

So Connie did what she does best; she talked to a lot of people. They in turn talked to more people. Phone calls were made, faxes were sent, feathers were ruffled. The result? Well, just one month after the original incident, American Hawaii added 2 disability specialists to their staff, and miraculously their discriminatory policies disappeared. People with disabilities are now free to cruise independently. Connie's client was able to take her honeymoon without having to be accompanied by a hearing person. But this didn't happen without a lot of public input. So, it never hurts to rock the boat a bit; in fact you might just be the impetus for some much needed change in the industry!!

Ships—Choosing a cruise ship is analogous to choosing a hotel; as it's where you'll live, sleep and play for the length of your holiday at sea. And although most cruise ships offer more amenities than hotels, they're of little use if you can't actually access them. For example, some of the ships built in the early to mid 90's have good access to most public areas, except for the spas. So, if you want to enjoy a facial or massage aboard these ships you'll be out of luck. Remember to ask about access to all areas of the ship. Suffice it to say, that thorough pre-trip research is an essential step in cruise planning. Remember, access can vary greatly from ship to ship, even on the same cruise line.

Generally speaking, the newer and larger ships offer the best access. The obvious exception to that rule is Renaissance Cruise Lines, which offers no accessible cabins. Try to stay away from the older ships that have been refurbished; as you'll find the best access on ships that were designed to be accessible, rather than those that were retrofitted.

A good place to start your research is at The Cruise Ship Center, a non-profit cruise portal at *www.cruise2.com*. Billed as a "free platform for buyers and sellers of cruises", The Cruise Ship Center has scads of helpful information including an updated list of accessible cabins. Cabin numbers of the accessible cabins are listed for every cruise ship, so it's a good place to bookmark. This website also contains other helpful information, such as ship profiles which list the age and size of each ship. Contact information for all the cruise lines is also listed on this site. This well organized site is a good general cruise resource, and a great place to start your research.

Once you've narrowed down your choices, contact the cruise lines directly, regarding access on each specific ship. Ask to speak to the special needs department or to an access specialist. This is the time to ask specific access questions about each ship. It should be noted that unofficially some of the cruise line's special needs agents "prefer" not to talk to clients directly. The reason given for this is that the clients "bog down the special needs agent with general cruise questions in addition to access questions." The general feeling seems to be that if the booking is later made through a travel agent, much of the information is duplicated. There is no official policy regarding this, but be aware you may encounter resistance from some special needs agents. If that happens, call back and speak to another agent, or take your business elsewhere.

When you contact the cruise line's special needs department, remember to ask very specific questions. As with everything else, don't just ask if the ship is accessible, or if the ship has accessible cabins. Ask specific questions about the access features of the ship. Inquiries regarding physical access are generally broken down into three main categories; the cabins, the bathrooms in the cabins, and the public areas of the ship. Make a worksheet for each ship and record the answers of the access specialist.

One of the first things to ask the access specialist is if they have any accessible cabins on the ship in question. But don't stop there. Ask how wide the doorway clearance to the cabin is, and if there is a sill or lip at the threshold. Some ships still have sizable lips; called coamings in nautical language. Ask about the dimensions of the cabin and request a detailed floor plan (which includes the measurements) of the accessible cabin. Don't forget to also ask about the width of the corridor outside of your cabin. It really doesn't matter how wide your cabin doorway is; if the outside corridor isn't wide enough for you to turn into the doorway.

If you use a power wheelchair or scooter, make sure the electrical supply on the ship is compatible with your battery charger. You may need to bring a electrical converter. Some cruise lines provide converters, but make sure (in advance) that it's compatible with your equipment. Additionally, since there are usually only one or two electrical outlets per cabin, consider packing an extension cord in case the outlet is out of reach of your wheelchair. You might also want to consider bringing a manual wheelchair along, as a backup and to use in some of the more inaccessible ports. If you do bring a manual wheelchair, make sure there is enough room in your cabin to store your power wheelchair or scooter. You cannot leave your scooter outside your cabin, so make sure there is enough room to maneuver your equipment in your cabin.

Next, you need to inquire about the bathroom in the accessible cabin. Ask for specific measurements, including the bathroom doorway clearance and the dimensions of the bathroom. Ask if there is a lip at the bathroom door. If so, ask if they provide a portable ramp. If a portable ramp is used, ask about the height of the bathroom lip. Do the math. A 1:12 grade means that you need one foot of ramp length for every inch of rise; so a six inch lip would require a six foot long ramp. Make sure there is enough room in the cabin to accommodate the ramp.

You also need to ask about the bathroom fixtures including the toilet and shower. Ask if there are toilet grab bars installed on the wall. Some cruise lines provide a raised toilet seat with grab bars attached to the seat. Although this configuration is preferred by people who have difficulty standing; it's unsuitable for wheelchair-users, as it makes lateral transfers impossible. Ask if the room has a roll-in shower or a tub-shower combination. If it has a roll-in shower ask if there is a fold down shower seat. If there is tub-shower combination, ask if they provide a portable shower seat.

If you need any special equipment, such as a commode chair or a shower chair, ask if the cruise line can provide it. Provide a detailed description, and even a photo of the type of equipment you need. Sometimes it's difficult to get the cruise lines to provide the proper equipment, so if you have very specific needs, it's best to bring your own equipment.

Finally, you need to inquire about the public areas of the ship. Ask about the width of the doorways leading to the outside decks, and if there are any sills (coamings) on the these doorways. Ask if there are any sills or lips on the doorways of any of the public rooms, including the public restrooms. Ask about the wheelchair seating in the showroom or theater. Some cruise lines seat wheelchair-users in the back (behind the last row of fixed seating) and make no allowance for companion seating. Ask if there is wheelchair access to all public areas of the ship, and inquire specifically about any area that is of particular interest to you. When you book your cruise, remember to request a table near the restaurant entrance, but out of the main traffic flow; as this will make for a more pleasant dining experience.

Accessible ground transportation is another important thing to consider. Unless you live in the port city, you will most likely arrive by air and require accessible ground transportation to and from the ship. If you purchase transfers from the cruise line, be sure and inform them that you need accessible transportation. Under the ADA, if a cruise line provides transportation to or from a US port, they must also provide an accessible option. Additionally, the cruise line cannot charge more for accessible transportation, even if it costs them more to provide this service. If the cruise line provides free transfers, they must also provide accessible transfers at no charge. According to the DOJ, "The ADA requires a cruise line to remove barriers in the facilities that they own or operate—including at U. S. ports-of-call, onboard ships (including guestrooms), and in transportation services." As previously mentioned, this also applies to foreign flag vessels which dock at US ports.

You can also opt to make arrangements for transfers on your own. Some travel agents are able to arrange transfers for you, but only if you book your cruise through them. Make sure you work with a travel agent that understands all the intricacies of accessible travel.

And if you do work with a travel agent, make sure that the cruise line debits your credit card directly. Why? Well, for one thing it protects you from the few unscrupulous agents who re-price cruises, doctor the tickets and then don't pass on the savings to their clients. It's not all that common but it does happen. If you pay the cruise line directly your agent won't be able to pocket any savings due you.

Second, if you pay the cruise line directly you'll be more protected from travel agencies that are "on the edge". I've come across a few agencies that offered huge discounts for prepayment to them (rather than the cruise lines). In short they loose money on the deal just to increase their cash flow. It goes without saying that any business that's willing to do that may be in dire financial trouble. You don't want to be left holding the bag, so it's best to avoid any agency that relies on this method to keep afloat financially. Remember, it's standard practice in the industry to have the cruise lines charge your credit card directly. Steer clear from anybody who claims otherwise.

Getting Off The Ship—Ship accessibility is only part of the equation when it comes to cruising, as disembarkation is another big concern. How do you get off the ship if you are in a wheelchair?. Do you just roll down the gangway? Well, sometimes that's the case, but often times it's a bit more complicated; as illustrated by the following comments from Bill, a first-time cruiser.

Says Bill of his cruise experience, "Last fall my wife and I cruised to Alaska on Princess Lines' *Crown Princess*. Although the ship was wonderfully accessible, and our cabin was complete with a roll-in shower; the ports themselves were lacking in accessibility. Many times I had to be carried off the ship in my wheelchair, by untrained personnel. At times I feared for my safety, not to mention the safety of my very expensive (and heavy) power wheelchair. I was also very embarrassed, as the rest of the passengers gathered around to see this 'spectacle'. I was told the ports were accessible, and not informed that I would have to be carried off the ship in this fashion."

Bill brings up a few good points. How do you find out if the ports have roll-off access? How do you know if you will be carried off the ship? Are there any other options? Basically there isn't one pat answer here. Although many cruise lines advise people that the ports are accessible this doesn't necessarily mean roll-off accessibility. As Princess cruise lines stated in reply to my inquiry on Bill's behalf, "Generally most ports are accessible to 'roll-off' with some help from our crew." In plain English that means you may be carried off the ship.

To be fair, Alaska does experience some drastic tidal fluctuations, so what is accessible one day will not necessarily be accessible the next. Sometimes you can roll-off, sometimes you will be carried off, sometimes cruise lines use a stair climber, and sometimes wheelchair-users can use the more level crew gangway. It all depends on the incline and access of the gangway, and what the cruise line considers the safest procedure for the conditions. The final decision on the safest procedure always lies with the captain of the ship. If the captain deems it too dangerous to carry off a passenger, then so be it. Basically, roll-off access is a roll of the dice.

Tendering, on the other hand is a much more straightforward procedure. Some ports are just not accessible to large ships, and sometimes even the larger ports are too crowded to allow all ships dockside access. In these cases, the ships must anchor offshore and tender their passengers to the docks. Tendering is the process of ferrying passengers by small boats, or tenders, from the cruise ship to the main dock. Most cruise lines can provide a list of tender ports, but depending on traffic and tide conditions, any port is a potential tender port.

Tendering is handled differently by the different cruise lines, but in most cases it involves hand carrying wheelchair-users onto the tender. Indeed, sometimes tendering can be a white knuckle experience, especially in rough seas. To eliminate this problem, Holland America Lines (HAL) recently developed an accessible alternative to this dangerous hand carrying procedure.

On September 25, 2000, HAL announced the debut of their new accessible tendering system. Appropriately named the Shore Tender Accessibility Project, this new system allows wheelchair-users to safely board tenders. The new system was designed by Cap Sante Marine, Inc. and includes a lift that runs on an inclined track from the top of the ship's gangway to the tender. A ramp on the tender then allows wheelchair-users to roll on board the tender. When the tender reaches the dock, a hydraulic leveling system adjusts for the height differences between the dock and the tender. This process gives wheelers roll-off access to the dock.

Previously, wheelchair-users had to be carried on and off of tenders. This new system allows wheelers to remain in their own wheelchair during the entire tendering process. HAL is the first cruise line to install this type of an accessible tendering system.

Currently this system is only available on the *ms Statendam*, but HAL also has plans to outfit the *ms Ryndam* and the *ms Volendam* with the accessible tendering system. Hopefully more cruise lines will follow suit to make tendering a safer procedure across the board.

Shore Excursions—Although many cruise lines are pretty forthcoming with information about their official shore excursions, most are rather tight lipped with information about port accessibility. They are even tighter lipped when it comes to information about the accessibility of their official shore excursions. At times, it seems like this information is a highly guarded state secret!!

For example, several years ago I contacted Princess Cruise Lines to inquire about the accessibility of their Alaska shore excursions. All I wanted to know was which shore excursions were accessible. It seemed a simple enough question. After dodging the issue for several months, Princess' official reply to my query was that this information would be available to me after I booked a cruise. So basically they told me that unless I booked a cruise they wouldn't even tell me if any of their shore excursions are accessible. That seemed unfair; after all most people like to know what they are buying before they write out the check. To be fair, Princess isn't alone here. It's like pulling teeth to get any access information about shore excursions out of the cruise lines. But, in retrospect that's not really a bad thing, because according to many veteran-cruisers, most of the information they eventually provide is often inaccurate.

In truth, there are only a handful of accessible shore excursions, so be wary if a cruise line indicates that a specific shore excursion is accessible. Make sure and ask a lot of questions, especially about the availability of accessible transportation. I've had reports from travelers who booked "accessible" shore excursions and arrived to find that non-lift equipped buses were part of the package. Replies from tour providers about their access deficits range from "it's only a few steps" to "once you get on the bus the rest of the tour is accessible." So, be forewarned that there is a very broad definition of "accessible" when it comes to shore excursions. Some tour providers assume that anybody in a wheelchair can walk at least a few steps; so what's accessible to them may not exactly be accessible to you.

So, what's a person to do when it comes to shore excursions? Basically you have two options. One is to work with a travel agent who is experienced in accessible travel, and have them plan your cruise and accessible shore excursions. The other option is to hit the books and plan your own accessible shore excursions. The one thing you shouldn't do is book your cruise with one travel agent and then contact another travel agent to plan your accessible shore excursions.

Most shore excursions are conducted by local tour operators. The cruise lines charge these operators a hefty percentage in order to add them to their official shore excursion list. So, the tour operators have to raise their prices in order to make a go of it. The end result? You pay higher prices for "official" shore excursions. Additionally, if something goes wrong on the shore excursion, the cruise line passes the buck to the tour operator. The cruise line's defense is that they contract out this service so the tour operator is ultimately responsible for the service.

Additionally, some cruise lines also offer commissions to travel agents for selling their official shore excursions. This results in many travel agents pushing the official shore excursions; even if they aren't accessible. So again, it's buyer-beware. If you are working with a travel agent who insists that all the shore excursions are accessible, ask for specific access details. Chances are they are just reciting cruise line rhetoric and they don't fully understand the real meaning of accessible.

If you go it on your own, the best tool for finding information on accessible shore excursions is the internet. If you don't have an internet connection, try logging on at a library. The reason the internet is such a good resource is that it allows you to connect directly with a local tour operator. Deal direct and save!! You'll also be able to get first hand access information if you deal direct, and it's a lot cheaper than faxing and phoning. Additionally if you don't speak the native language, there are many free translation programs available that allow you to translate you e-mail messages to the native tongue. You should also be aware that some local providers don't take credit cards, so it may be hard to get a refund if the appropriate services aren't provided.

Once you're connected to the internet, you have to act like a detective. You can't just go to a search engine and type in "accessible cruise excursions" and expect results. Do a search under "accessible travel" and look for contacts in your port cities. Another good source of information can be disability organizations. Make a list of your port cities and post messages on travel bulletin boards for information on access. Search for destination related resources and then find out if they have any access information. Contact tourist bureaus to see if they have any access information.

Many smaller tour companies are willing to work with tourists to create specialized tours. Seek out these local companies. Join e-mail lists, search disability web sites and ask anybody and everybody if they have any information or contacts. You never know when one person may be the key to your search. It really is a numbers game—ask enough people and eventually you will get the answers you need. Be sure and allow plenty of time for your research, as results don't magically materialize overnight. Like anything else, you have to work at it.

Once you've found a local tour operator, be sure to allow some leeway when scheduling your tour. On many cruise lines, passengers booked on the official shore excursions get first crack at the tenders. Be sure and inform the tour operator of your need for flexibility with the time frame. Make sure this is understood before you book your tour. Another option is to find accessible transportation and see the port on your own. Sometimes this is a better solution if you feel you will be pressed for time. This way you can see the sights and go back to the ship at your leisure. Sometimes this is the best option for short port stops.

Destinations—Just as cruise ships vary in accessibility, so do destinations. Generally speaking some destinations are just more accessible than others. As far as cruising goes, Alaska is by far the most accessible destination. There are many reasons for this, including the fact that many of the tourist sites have been made accessible in order to comply with the ADA. There is also a greater availability of accessible transportation in Alaska. Some of the cruise lines even own accessible buses, which they use for some shore excursions. Finding access information is easier too. First off, the language isn't a barrier. Second, there are many CILs and disability organizations to choose from. And third, it's pretty well touristed by wheelchair-users, so local businesses seem to be aware of access issues. Here are a few details on the Alaska port cities of Ketchikan, Juneau, and Skagway.

Much of Ketchikan is built on a hillside, but Saxman Totem Park has limited accessibility for guests using wheelchairs or scooters. As one traveler puts it, "it's do-able for wheelchair-users, but it requires strong arms, or somebody to push your wheelchair." Also recommended is the Southeast Visitors Center, which is just a short walk from the dock. It features great accessibility and interesting displays, plus you can do it on your own. The whale watching tours are not accessible, even though some cruise lines indicate otherwise. The only way to board the whale watching boats is to be carried on board.

Walking in Juneau also presents some difficulties, due to the steep hillsides. Accessible attractions include a dockside cultural center, which features Alaska native crafts, the Gastineau Fish Hatchery and the spectacular (and very accessible) Mount Roberts Aerial Tramway. ERA Helicopters (800-843-1947) also offers accessible flightseeing tours over the nearby glaciers. Advance reservations are a must for this popular attraction.

The town of Skagway is only about four blocks square, and it's not too strenuous for wheelchair-users. Transportation on lift-equipped shuttle buses is available for about $1 per person. The White Horse Yukon Railroad is very accessible and offers dramatic scenery. This is a must-see for train buffs. The railway has lifts for accessible boarding and wheelchair tie-downs. Overall, Alaska is one of the most accessible cruise destinations; however be prepared for varied methods of ship disembarkation due to the fluctuating tides.

The Caribbean is another story altogether, in regards to access. In short, access in the Caribbean is troublesome in most places. Be ready to compromise on access if this is your dream destination. Although accessible transportation is still limited in many places, it's available now in Bermuda, Puerto Rico, the Bahamas, St. Thomas, St. Croix, Barbados and St. Vincent. Accessible transportation providers are listed in the resource chapter. Be sure and make your arrangements for accessible transportation well in advance. Also, don't forget to contact the CILs as a resource in the US Virgin Islands and Puerto Rico.

And then there's Europe. Although Europe isn't very good for access on large cruise ships, there's a wide variety of accessible options on the smaller river boats. Europe just can't compare to Alaska for an accessible cruise experience. Two time cruiser Tim, sums it up best with comments about his *Crown Princess* cruise to Europe. "I really wanted to see Europe," he recalls, "but I was very disappointed with my Princess Cruise experience. They told me they had accessible shore excursions, but they didn't. It was a real struggle in every port. They did give me some access information, but it was very outdated. In retrospect, I would have been better off on a barge or river cruise. It was quite a disappointment, compared to my cruise experience in Alaska."

Barges and Narrow Boats—From barges to river boats, small ship cruising continues to grow in popularity throughout the world. Although there are a few barge and river boat cruise companies in the US, none of the ships are very accessible. Some companies do have cabins that they sell as accessible, but first person reports on access abroad these vessels has been very dismal. So for now, if you want to try cruising on a smaller vessel, it's best to turn to Europe for the best access. Here are a few suggestions. All contact information is listed in the resource chapter.

Cruise the canals of Northwest England on board *New Horizons*, an accessible canal (narrow) boat. *New Horizons* is operated by the Stockport Canalboat Trust, and staffed with a skipper and volunteer crew. Stockport Canalboat Trust offers accessible day trips and short canal holidays on board *New Horizons*. *New Horizons* features a boarding ramp and lift, plus wheelchair access throughout the boat.

Two accessible canal boats, the *Madam Butterfly* and the *Dawn*; are available for hire on the Bassingstoke Canal in England. The *Dawn* is a day-use boat which can accommodate 12 passengers. It has lift access and an accessible toilet. The *Madam Butterfly*, a larger boat, has seven berths, one cabin with a hospital bed, lift access, hoists, and an accessible toilet and shower. Both boats are operated by the "Boats for the Handicapped Association," a UK charity.

The Lyneal Trust provides accessible canal boat holidays on the Llangollen Canal, from their base at the Lyneal Wharf (near Ellesmere). This UK charity operates 2 accessible canal boats, the *Shropshire Lass* and the *Shropshire Lad*. The *Shropshire Lass* is a 70 foot residential canal boat which sleeps eight, and the *Shropshire Lad* is a 45 foot canal boat designed for day trips. The Lyneal Wharf also houses accessible lodging for up to 16 people.

Cruise the waterways of Ireland on the *Saoirse ar an Uisce* (Freedom on the Water). This fully equipped barge has central heating, a full galley and can sleep up to eight people. The barge is accessible to wheelchair-users via a boarding ramp. This is a "self drive barge", but there are also skippers available for hire if you prefer to leave the driving to somebody else.

The 110 passenger *MV Dresden* makes weekly cruises between Hamburg and Dresden on the Elbe River in Eastern

Germany. There is one wheelchair-accessible cabin, with a roll-in shower. This riverboat was built in 1991 and refurbished in 1996. All public rooms are barrier-free except for the gift shop and the beauty shop

And finally, you might want to consider a French barge holiday. Le Boat, Inc. operates accessible barges on the Midi, Digoin and Nivernais canals of France. If you prefer to leave the driving to somebody else, they also have a wheelchair accessible barge with full service and a crew. Says one veteran barger, "if you think a trip to Europe won't be accessible enough for you, then barging may be the way to go. Floating slowly through the canals of France was a very accessible and a totally enjoyable experience for me!"

9 | When Things Go Wrong

Anybody who tells you that your travels will be trouble-free is either a liar or a fool. There are no guarantees in life, and travel by its very nature is unpredictable. There are numerous variables involved on any given trip, and theoretically something could go awry at any stage of the game. Add accessibility issues to this equation and your odds of experiencing a travel mishap greatly increase. I'm not trying to scare you or discourage you. I'm just trying to prepare you. Expect something to go wrong at some point in your travels. It may not happen on your first trip; it may not even happen on your second trip. But odds are it will happen. So the best defense is proper preparation.

One of the best ways to prepare for your trip is by playing a healthy game of "what if" before you depart. Ask yourself questions like "what if my wheelchair breaks while I'm on vacation?" Having some well thought out solutions to these "what if" scenarios will come in very handy when disaster strikes. For example, a good solution to the previous "what if" question would be to gather the phone numbers of a few wheelchair repair shops in your destination city. Of course it's easy to go overboard with the "what if" game. Remember I said a "healthy" game of "what if". Sometimes there is a fine line between obsession and preparation. Try not to cross over the line.

So, what do you do when disaster strikes while you are on the road? Well, your immediate goal should be to solve the problem, and salvage your vacation. Next you should try to mitigate or prevent further damage. Sometimes these two goals overlap, and sometimes they even conflict with one another. For example if your wheelchair is damaged, you first priority should be to make it useable so you won't have to cancel the remaining portion of your trip. However, if using your chair "as is" could cause further damage, it's best to sacrifice a few days of your trip in order to get it properly repaired. In the end it's a judgment call on your part.

You will also have to learn how to effectively communicate your needs to customer service personnel. For example, if your power wheelchair is damaged, you most likely will have to explain to airline personnel why a manual wheelchair is not an appropriate loaner. Try not to loose your temper, although admittedly that's difficult when dealing with morons. Threatening to sue or file a formal complaint at this point, never really helps. It just creates an adversarial situation. Concentrate on maintaining your composure, and try to calmly explain your needs. It also helps to explain the reasons behind your needs; in other words tell the clerk why you can't use a manual chair. In the long run this is usually the quickest way to an appropriate resolution. Sometimes this is easier said than done.

You may also want to address your financial loss at the time of the incident. Bear in mind, you may not get a final resolution to this matter, but at least you will have set the ball in motion. You may get an upgrade or some other minor perk for your troubles. Not that I'm implying that a first class upgrade is payment enough for a mangled wheelchair, but if an upgrade it offered on-the-spot, take it. If you later learn your actual damages are substantial, you can address that problem when you get home. Be sure and keep all documentation of your actual damages, such as extra hotel nights and airline cancellation charges. Many companies will reimburse you, simply because it's a good public relations move. In any case, when you ask for compensation, be realistic. If your trip was delayed for one day and you had to pay a $75 cancellation penalty to re-book your flight, don't ask for

$1500. You have a much better chance of receiving prompt compensation if you demands are realistic.

Save your official complaints for when you get home. Do remember to collect documentation along the way, save receipts and get names. You might also want to jot down the details of the incident, while they're fresh in your mind. Then, go away on your vacation and try to enjoy yourself. I know this is easier said then done, but there's no sense ruining your trip any more over an unfortunate incident. Dwelling on the matter won't accomplish anything. When you get home, you can start the official complaint process. Most likely there won't be a swift resolution to your official complaint, and in some cases it won't even be acknowledged. After all, we are talking about government agencies here.

So why take the time to file a official complaint? In most cases this is the only way to enforce US access laws, and to effect change. Filing an official complaint is a very personal decision; but, you must also realize that access won't improve until more people come forward and complain. Although many agencies don't respond to individual complaints, they do look at trends. So, if a particular business is getting a lot of the same type of complaints, there is a chance the enforcement agency will look into it. The first step in filing a official complaint is determining where and how to file it. This varies and depends upon the nature of your complaint.

Air Travel—The Air Carriers Access Act (ACAA) covers all aspects of airline travel on US based air carriers. The enforcement agency for the ACAA is the Department of Transportation (DOT). A common misconception shared by many people is that air travel is covered under the American with Disabilities Act (ADA). It is not. Air travel on US carriers is addressed in the ACAA, which was established in 1986 and actually predates the ADA. I stress this fact because you need to know the law in order to advocate for yourself. If you spout off to an airline employee that you are unhappy with their service and that you are going to file an ADA complaint, you will only prove your ignorance. The airlines know the rules better than most of us, so you need to be educated on the law, in order to be taken seriously.

Although there is much debate about the effectiveness of the ACAA, it does offer some protection and many essential services to people with disabilities. One of the most useful mandates of the ACAA is the creation of the Complaints Resolution Official (CRO). All US carriers must have a CRO available 24 hours a day to specifically address alleged ACAA violations and to solve customer complaints. The CRO is an airline employee specifically trained in airline duties and passenger rights under the ACAA. The CRO may be available either in person or by phone. So, if you encounter a problem en route in regards to a violation of the ACAA, and you can't solve the problem with front line personnel, ask to speak to the CRO immediately. It's your right, and the first step you should take to resolve your problem on-the-spot. Bear in mind that the gate agent or ticket agent may not know who or what the CRO is, especially if they are new employees. In that case, just ask to speak to a supervisor. Anybody in a supervisory position should be very well educated on the role of the CRO.

Interestingly enough, CROs technically also have authority over third party contractors. This is important to remember because many airlines use third party contractors as wheelchair pushers (in the airport) and for assisting non-ambulatory passengers with boarding and deplaning. When a problem arises with one of these services, airline employees may claim there is nothing they can do because the service is provided by a third party contractor. According to section 382.9 of the ACAA, all airline contracts with third party providers must include a clause that states, "contractor employers will comply with directives issued by CROs." So the next time you have a problem with a third party contractor, make sure and point out this often-overlooked section of the ACAA to the CRO.

You can also file a written complaint with the airline after you return home. This is your best (and sometimes only) route to monetary compensation for damages. Do watch your time limit here though, as airlines are not required to respond to complaints postmarked more than 45 days after the violation. For complaints filed in a timely manner, the airline must respond in 30 days. You also have the right to file an official complaint with the DOT at any time. Additionally you can just skip the airline and go right to the DOT and file an official complaint.

The official DOT complaint process is pretty easy. It consists of filling out a simple form and returning it to the DOT. Alternatively you can submit a letter outlining the details of the incident to the DOT at address listed below. Personally I recommend using the complaint form, as the specific questions are designed to gather pertinent information that is often overlooked or omitted. You can get a copy of the complaint form on-line in PDF format at *www.dot.gov/airconsumer/ complaints1.htm*, or contact the DOT.

Department of Transportation
Aviation Consumer Protection Division, C-75-D
400 Seventh St., SW
Washington DC 2059
(202) 366-2220

Don't expect an answer or acknowledgment to your complaint. Because of the volume of complaints, the DOT tends to address trends, rather than individual complaints. Still, don't let this discourage your from submitting a complaint, as it is the only way to effect change. In any case, if your complaint is addressed you will not receive any monetary compensation for your losses. DOT complaints usually result in an adjustment to airline policies and practices. They do not include monetary compensation for damages to the complainant. You must address this issue directly with the airline (within the required time period).

And finally, when dealing with violations of the ACAA, you may have some slight redress for monetary damages through a civil lawsuit. Of course you are always free to sue anybody you choose; however, you may have problems finding an attorney to take an ACAA case on a contingency basis. There are no real provisions in the ACAA for the recovery of legal fees, so it may be hard to find an attorney that will take a case on a contingency arrangement. Most likely you will have to pay a retainer up front and then continue to pay hourly costs every month. This could become quite expensive, and technically it's not a recoverable cost. I say technically because the August 1999 amendment to the ACAA allows for consequential damages in cases of wheelchair damage. Could consequential damages be interpreted as legal costs? Time will tell, as this most likely will be decided by precedent. For now though, civil litigation is a costly and somewhat ineffective way to deal with ACAA violations.

Airports—It would be nice if there was one federal agency or department set aside to deal with access in US airports. This however is not the case, as the presiding enforcement agency is dependent upon many factors; including when the airport was built, where it is located and what type of funds were used to construct the facility. It's also not uncommon to have different areas within the same facility fall under the jurisdiction of different enforcement agencies. It's confusing at best, but here's the basic rundown of how it all works.

Airports that receive federal funding are subject to Section 504 of the Rehabilitation Act of 1973, and the implementing regulations developed by the Department of Transportation (DOT). However, airports that are owned or operated by state or local governments (considered public entities) are subject to Title II of the ADA. This regulation applies even if the airport in question also receives federal funding. Title II also covers any fixed route transportation system (such as airport parking shuttles) within a public entity airport. Complaints addressing violations to either of these regulations may be filed with the Federal Aviation Administration at the address listed below. For more information call (202) 267-3270.

Federal Aviation Administration
Office of Civil Rights (ACR-4)
800 Independence Avenue, SW
Washington DC 20591

Privately owned public-use airports are subject to Title III of the ADA. Violations found in these facilities should be addressed to the Department of Justice (DOJ) at the following address. For more information call 800-514-0301.

Disability Rights Section
Civil Rights Division
US Department of Justice
PO Box 66738
Washington DC 20035-6738

And finally, all terminal facilities owned, leased or operated by an air carrier at a commercial airport are subject to provisions in the ACAA. See the "Air Travel" section for details on how to address an ACAA complaint.

Ground Transportation—Ground transportation accessibility is covered under the ADA. In regards to enforcement of the law, ground transportation is divided into two categories; publicly owned transportation and privately owned transportation. Access standards for public transportation in the US are mandated under Title II of the ADA. For the purpose of this discussion, public transportation includes city bus lines, paratransit services, commuter rail lines, subways and Amtrack. The US Access Board developed the access guidelines for public transportation mandated under Title II of the ADA; and public transportation authorities must follow these guidelines and adhere to the accessibility requirements for newly purchased vehicles.

The Federal Transit Administration (FTA), a division of the DOT, provides for enforcement of Title II of the ADA with respect to public transportation. You can obtain a complaint form on the

FTA website at *www.fta.dot.gov/office/civil/adacf.htm* or call the FTA ADA Assistance Line at (888) 446-4511 for more information. Mail you completed complaint to the FTA office at the address listed below.

> Director
> FTA Office of Civil Rights
> 400 7th Street, SW, Room 9102
> Washington DC 20590

Privately owned vehicles, such as those owned by hotels and private bus companies are covered under Title III of the ADA. Title III complaints should be directed to the DOJ at the following address. For more information call (800) 514-0301.

> Disability Rights Section
> Civil Rights Division
> US Department of Justice
> PO Box 66738
> Washington DC 20035-6738

You may also enforce your rights under Title II and Title III of the ADA through a private lawsuit. Provisions in the ADA allow for the payment of reasonable legal expenses on Title II and Title III cases. Because of these provisions it's much easier to get an attorney or an advocacy organization to take a Title II or Title III case on a contingency basis. This makes private lawsuits a realistic solution for many people, but unfortunately it also opens up the door for legal malpractice. Always use great care when choosing a attorney.

Cruise Ships—Technically, cruise ships are covered under the ADA. Realistically, compliance is difficult to enforce in this area. The reason for this difficulty is that the US Access Board has not yet established any accessibility standards for cruise ships. Look for that to change in the next few years though, as the US Access Board is currently working to remedy this matter. The US Access Board is responsible for developing accessibility guidelines under the ADA; and the Passenger Vessel Access Advisory Committee was created in order to make recommendations for the final guidelines.

The Passenger Vessel Access Advisory Committee completed their work in December 2000, when they submitted their recommendations to the US Access Board. These recommendations are currently under review by the US Access Board. Once a proposed rule is developed by the US Access Board, it will be submitted to the Office of Management and Budget (OMB) for review. This can take up to 90 days. The proposed rule is then published in the Federal Register. At this time the proposed rule is open for public comment, usually for a period of 60 days. After the public comment period ends, the US Access Board takes another four to six months to review the comments and modify the rule. The final rule goes back to the OMB for review, which takes up to 90 days. The final rule is then published in the Federal Register, and can either take effect immediately or at specified time in the future (i.e.: in 30 days or on a specific date).

So, as you can see, even though the rule making process has begun, it may still be a while before the official rule is on the books. Once the regulations are developed, passenger vessels operated by private entities (most cruise ships) will fall under Title III of the ADA, while passenger vessels operated by state and local governments (some ferries) will fall under Title II. Even though most cruise ships are not US registered, the final rule will most likely cover all ships which call on US ports. For now, any access provided by non-US registered cruise ships is somewhat voluntary on their part. For more information on US Access Board activities, including updates of the Passenger Vessel Access Advisory Committee, visit the US Access Board website at *www.access-board.gov*. The US Access Board also publishes

Access Currents, a free bimonthly newsletter. Call (202) 272-5434 to subscribe.

Hotels, Restaurants and Tourist Attractions—The lion's share of tourist facilities fall under this category, and most are covered either under Title II or Title III of the ADA. Title III covers public accommodations; those facilities which are privately owned but open to the general public. This includes privately owned hotels, restaurants, bars, theaters, recreation areas, museums and tourist attractions. Title III of the ADA is enforced by the DOJ, and complaints should be sent to the address listed below.

Disability Rights Section
Civil Rights Division
US Department of Justice
Post Office Box 66738
Washington DC 20035-6738

There is no official Title III complaint form, so just submit a signed letter which details the alleged ADA violation. Remember to include all pertinent information such as dates, names and addresses. You may also include other documentation, such as receipts and photos, with your letter. Never send original receipts or documentation, as they won't be returned to you and you may need them for future action. For more information call (800) 514-0301.

Title II of the ADA covers access to services, programs, activities, facilities and buildings owned or operated by state or local governments. This could include facilities such as state owned museums, recreation areas or tourist attractions. Additionally if you are unlucky enough to end up in a local or country court (watch those speed traps!); those facilities are also covered under Title II. You can get a copy of the Title II complaint form on the DOJ website at *www.usdoj.gov/crt/ada/publicat.htm*.

Return the completed form to the address below. For more information call 800-514-0301.

Disability Rights Section
Civil Rights Division
US Department of Justice
Post Office Box 66738
Washington DC 20035-6738

You may also enforce your rights under Title II and Title III of the ADA through a private lawsuit. Provisions in the ADA allow for the payment of reasonable legal expenses on Title II and Title III cases. Many advocacy organizations that specialize in disability rights law will either help you put your case together, or represent you outright. Alternatively, you may hire a disability rights attorney of your choice to litigate this matter for you.

National Parks—There's a lot of confusion out there about access requirements for US National Parks. There is also a lot of misinformation. You may have heard that the ADA does not cover access in US National Parks. This is true; however, some people interpret this fact to mean that US National Parks are not required to be accessible. This is untrue. US National Parks are required to be accessible. Access in US National Parks is covered under Section 504 of the Rehabilitation Act of 1973; legislation that actually predates the ADA. Additionally, concessionaires in US National Parks are responsible for providing appropriate access to all programs, services and facilities. This is important to remember as many US National Parks have concessionaires who provide lodging, food and tour services. The National Parks Service (NPS) is ultimately responsible if these concessionaires are in violation of any access laws.

So, where do you go if you encounter an access problem in a US National Park? Common sense would tell you to talk to the Access Coordinator for the park; and that's fine if you just want to talk about access. The Access Coordinator is actually a NPS employee, and although he may be interested in access solutions, he's not in any position to implement them. Consider the Access Coordinator something akin to an access advisor; he merely makes recommendations. Many Access Coordinators have great ideas and are very helpful. But when it comes to action, most don't have enough influence to actually facilitate access improvements. Access mandates come from above; and they are usually the result of official complaints.

Official complaints should be directed to the Department of the Interior at the address listed below. Write a letter describing your access problem and state that you are making an official complaint under Section 504 of the Rehabilitation Act of 1973. Try to be as inclusive and detailed as possible when describing your access problem. Send you complaint to the following address or call (202) 208-5694 for more information.

> US Department of the Interior
> Office of Equal Opportunity
> Director
> 1849 C St. NW, MS-5214
> Washington DC 20240-0002

Technical assistance and general information about access in US National Parks can also be obtained by calling the National Center on Accessibility's Technical Assistance Line at (812) 856-4422. The National Center on Accessibility has done a great deal of work in this area, and they are really the experts. They also have a very informative website at *www.ncaonline.org*.

Often Overlooked Laws—Many people think only of the ADA when addressing access violations in the US; however, the ADA is far from the only law mandating access. It's one of the newer access laws, and perhaps that's why it gets so much press. In truth, many laws actually predate the ADA, and sometimes these useful laws are overlooked when addressing access violations. It pays to be on the lookout for all access laws that may apply to your particular case; and remember, sometimes more than one law may apply. Here are a few often overlooked access laws you might want to consider.

The Architectural Barriers Act of 1968 (ABA) mandates accessibility in certain buildings financed or leased by the federal government. Buildings that were constructed or altered with federal funds may be subject to this legislation. The key words here are "federal funds", so follow the money trail to determine if a building falls under ABA jurisdiction. The current access standards for the ABA are detailed in the Uniform Federal Accessibility Standards. The US Access Board is responsible for enforcement of the ABA, and all complaints should be directed to the address below. For technical assistance call (800) 872-2253.

US Access Board
1331 F St., NW, Suite 1000
Washington DC 20004-1111

If the US Access Board determines there is a violation of the ABA, they will notify the responsible agency and request the removal of access barriers. The US Access Board monitors the progress of the removal, and updates the complainant of the status. In rare cases, the US Access Board has sought court action to enforce ABA violations; but that's usually not necessary as the US Access Board has an excellent record of achieving voluntary compliance.

Another often overlooked access law is Section 504 of the Rehabilitation Act of 1973. Although I touched on this law briefly is some earlier sections in this chapter, be aware there are many avenues to enforce Section 504. Section 504 states that no qualified person with a disability shall be denied access to programs or services that receive federal financial assistance. So, once again, follow the money trail to determine if your access problem is covered under this law. The confusing part about

Section 504 is that each federal agency has it's own set of 504 regulations that apply to their particular programs. Each department also has it's own contact person, and Section 504 complaints must be filed with the appropriate federal agency. Section 504 complaints can also be pursued in civil court. For information on how to file a Section 504 complaint with the appropriate agency, contact the DOJ at the address below or call (800) 514-0301.

> Disability Rights Section
> Civil Rights Division
> US Department of Justice
> PO Box 66738
> Washington DC 20035-6738

Finally, don't overlook any state or local civil rights laws that may pertain to your access complaint. For example, in California, the Unruh Civil Rights Act prohibits businesses from discriminating against certain individuals, including people with a disability. So, a California tourist attraction would be in violation of the Unruh Civil Rights Act if it charged people with a disability a higher admission price, or even refused them access or entrance to their establishment. Many states have some type of civil rights legislation that may pertain to discrimination against people with a disability. Check with your State Office of Civil Rights for more information.

Lawyers and Court—Since Title II and Tittle III cases provide for the payment of reasonable legal fees, more and more attorneys are willing to take these types of cases on a contingency basis. In fact, many law offices actively solicit these types of cases, through fancy websites and slick disability rights pamphlets. Although I'm all in favor of the distribution of accurate disability rights information, be forewarned that you do need to exercise some caution when searching for an attorney to represent you.

First and foremost, always remember that you are the boss, even if you don't pay your lawyer any money up front. The attorney you hire is working for you, even if you have a contingency arrangement. Some attorneys may imply that they are taking your case (at no cost to you) out of the kindness of their heart. Remember, they will recover their expenses and fees if they win the case. It's also not unusual for attorney fees to sometimes exceed the plaintiff's award. Just keep things in perspective, and remain in control of your legal proceedings. Your lawyer works for you.

And a few words about choosing an attorney; be careful. Obviously you shouldn't choose an attorney just because he will take your case on a contingency basis. Ask for references and ask what types of disability rights cases he has tried in the past. Try and find an attorney who has experience with cases that are similar to yours. "Disability rights" is a very broad category. And finally, don't be afraid to ask your attorney what percentage of disability rights cases he has won. If the cases are closed, the settlements should be a matter of public record, so also ask him for specific case names. Spend some time selecting your attorney, and don't let anybody rush you into a decision.

Alternatively. you can represent yourself, and file your own Pro Se ADA Complaint in Federal District Court. The Pennsylvania Coalition of Citizens with Disabilities has compiled some easy-to-understand instructions along with the forms required to file your own complaint. You can find these on the internet at *www.ragged-edge-mag.com/archive/pro-se.htm.* If you need further assistance or have any questions about the process, contact the Pennsylvania Coalition of Citizens with Disabilities at (717) 238-0172.

For More Information—There's a lot of good information available about disability rights legislation. Here are a few of my favorite resources.

Air Carrier Access: This free guide is published by the Eastern Paralyzed Veterans Association. It explains consumer rights and airline responsibilities under the ACAA in simple language. It also includes some good photographs of airline boarding procedures for non-ambulatory passengers. A good primer on the ACAA.

Eastern Paralyzed Veterans Association
75-20 Astoria Blvd.
Jackson Heights, NY 11370-1177
(800) 444-0120

The Americans with Disabilities Act Your Personal Guide to the Law: Published by the Paralyzed Veterans of America, this 53 page booklet contains general information on the different titles of the Americans with Disabilities Act. Information about enforcement and tax incentives is also included.

Paralyzed Veterans of America
801 Eighteenth St., NW
Washington DC 20006
(800) 424-8200

A Guide to Disability Rights Laws: This 17 page guide presents a good overview of eight federal access laws. Laws covered include the ADA, ABA, the Rehabilitation Act of 1973 and the ACAA. This free guide also contains a helpful list of disability rights resources.

Consumer Information Center
Pueblo, CO 81009
(888) 878-3256

10 | Beyond The USA

Access doesn't magically disappear once you venture beyond US borders; however, it does change. These changes can be good or bad, depending on your perspective. With that in mind, there are a number of things to consider if a foreign destination is on your travel calendar.

First off, you should become familiar with the access laws of your destination country. The US is not the only country that has rules and regulations which govern access; in fact, some countries have even stricter laws with higher access standards. It's true that the Americans with Disabilities Act (ADA) won't protect you on foreign soil; however, don't rule out the existence of local access laws. Of course, some countries are at the other end of the access spectrum; and have no human rights or access legislation. Whatever the case, it pays to find out about the laws (or the lack of laws) before you hit the road. This helps you understand local customs; and, more importantly, gives you a good idea of what to expect in the access department.

Canada—Because of its proximity to the US, Canada is a popular destination for many Americans. Canada presents a welcome air of familiarity, as English is widely spoken throughout the country. But, there are many differences too. As far as access laws go, it's a fifty-fifty split; some are very familiar and some are drastically different. Here's a breakdown of what to expect.

On the strikingly familiar side, is the Canadian Transportation Act of 1996 (CTA), which covers access on transportation throughout Canada. Among other things, the CTA mandates access at airports and on Canadian airlines (on aircraft with 30 or more seats). The air transportation regulations under the CTA are very much like our own Air Carriers Access Act (ACAA). Basically the regulations mandate access and prohibit disability-based discrimination at Canadian airports or on Canadian airlines. So although Americans are not protected by the ACAA on Canadian airlines, most travelers feel comfortable with the protection afforded them under the CTA air transportation regulations. For more information on the CTA, or for a copy of the CTA air transportation regulations, contact the Accessible Transportation Directorate at the Canadian Transportation Agency in Ottawa. An electronic version of the CTA air transportation regulations is also available on-line at *www.cta-otc.gc.ca/access/regs/air_e.html.*

There are also some glaring differences in Canadian access laws and standards. For example, even though disability-based discrimination is prohibited under the Canadian Human Rights Act of 1976-77; there are no building codes which address physical access. This results in much confusion for uninformed Americans who assume that Canadian access standards are the same as those mandated under the ADA. They are not. In fact, there is no disability legislation in Canada which actually regulates physical access to buildings.

In order to address this problem, the Hotel Association of Alberta founded Access Canada; a voluntary rating program for Canadian hotels and motels. The Access Canada rating system is divided into four levels; with level four having the highest level of access. Level one has basic pathway access while level four requires properties to have a roll-in shower and a trapeze bar over the bed. In truth there are very few level four properties.

Participating establishments are inspected by an Access Canada specialist to determine their access rating. After inspection, the property can then display the Access Canada logo along with their access rating. Although not widely used in

Canada, Access Canada is the only official access rating system for Canadian hotels; so it's a good idea to become familiar with it. Most of the Access Canada properties are located in Alberta and Victoria. For more information about Access Canada, visit the Alberta Hotel Association website at *www.albertahotels.ab.ca.*

In the absence of official access regulations, sometimes it's best to take the cue from disability organizations within the country. What do they consider accessible when it comes to hotel rooms? Well, here's the access criteria that the Canadian disability organization Keroul uses to define an adapted room.

"Accessible entrance is ground level or gently sloped, the threshold is less than two cm. high and the door is wider than 76 cm. The bathroom has a door at least 76 cm. wide, enough space to circulate (1.5 m. by 1.5 m.), grab bars and enough clearance under the wash basin (68.5 cm. or more). If there is one bedroom, it is large enough to move around in easily."

As you can see, it's not exactly an ADA definition of accessible; but it's pretty much what you can expect to find when you see that little blue wheelchair symbol in Canada. One final note about access in Canada; roll-in showers are not as commonplace as they are in the US. It's somewhat unusual to find a property that has a roll-in shower; so even if a property touts its "accessible bathroom"; be forewarned that a roll-in shower is probably not considered part of the access package. Remember to always ask specific questions about access. Never assume anything.

Europe—Europe is another popular vacation spot. The good news is that travelers can expect to find a high degree of access in most western European countries. On the other hand, there are a few differences between access in Europe and access in the US. It goes without saying that it pays to be aware of those differences. For purposes of clarity, when talking about access it's usually best to divide Europe up into two parts; the United Kingdom and continental Europe.

In 1995, Britain passed the Disability Discrimination Act (DDA), which made it illegal for providers of goods, services and facilities to discriminate against any person with a disability. The DDA applies to public accommodations such as hotels, airports and entertainment venues as well as to most transportation providers. It's important to note that the DDA excludes domestic air carriers in Britain. Domestic air carriers can voluntarily provide accessible services, but they are not required to do so. This point is well illustrated by the following tale of Disability Rights Commission Chief, Bert Massie.

Bert ran into some problems at London City airport, when he tried to board a Scot Airways flight to Edinburgh in late 2000. Massie, who uses a wheelchair, checked in for his flight, went through security, and proceeded to the gate. He was later told by the gate agent that he couldn't board the plane if he wasn't able to walk. Mr. Massie tried to make the best of the situation and offered to crawl up the three steps to the aircraft, or to have a friend carry him on board. Scot Airways refused his requests.

Merlin Suckling, Scot Airways' director and owner claims that "it's a well-publicized policy that Scot Airways does not allow wheelchair-bound people to fly on its planes." Well-publicized or not, there's no mention of that policy anywhere on the Scot Airways website. The bottom line is, (unfortunately) Scot Airways was operating within the law. Yes, it would have been nice for Scott Airways to notify Mr. Massie (before he bought his ticket) that they wouldn't be able to accommodate his needs; but, I expect that's a customer service issue. In any case, some British domestic carriers do accommodate people with disabilities; but again, this is a voluntary service. Remember to ask a lot of questions regarding access before booking any domestic flights within the United Kingdom. Make sure you will be able to get on and off the plane!

As far as accessible lodging goes, the UK uses the Tourism For All access rating system. This program works much like the Access Canada program. Properties are first inspected by a trained professional in order to determine their access rating. This rating is then noted in guide books, tourism department publications, lodging brochures and travel websites.

There are three categories in the Tourism For All access rating system; with category one having the highest level of access. Here's a quick breakdown of the Tourism for All rating categories.

- Category One: Accessible to an independent wheelchair user.
- Category Two: Accessible to a wheelchair user with assistance.
- Category Three: Accessible to someone with mobility difficulties, but able to walk up a minimum of three steps.

Roll-in (no rim) showers are required in all Category One and Category Two properties, which have a "shower only" (rather than a tub or a tub and shower combination). Please note, even though the Tourism For All access rating system is a voluntary program, it's widely used throughout the UK.

Another unique thing about access in the UK is the availability of accessible public toilets. The good news is that there are thousands of accessible public toilets throughout the UK. The bad news? They are locked, are only accessible with a National Key Scheme (NKS) key. NKS keys are available to the public; but you do have to plan ahead. Make sure you get the appropriate NKS keys before you leave home.

Britain's NKS covers over 5,000 accessible public toilets throughout the UK, and the best place for visitors to get their NKS key is from The Royal Association for Disability and Rehabilitation (RADAR). The cost is £2.50. RADAR also has a NKS guide that lists the locations of the accessible public toilets. It's available for £5.00. If your travels include the Republic of Ireland, a different key is available from the Access Department of the National Rehabilitation Board in Dublin. This key will open 99% of the locked accessible public toilets in the Republic.

Although there are lots of resources for travel to the UK, very few deal with access issues. The exception is Ann Litt's Undiscovered Britain website, which includes information about access to the theater, driving, the NKS toilets and lodging in Britain. Ann is a destination specialist for the UK, and she's an expert on all things British, including access. You can find her informative website at *www.UndiscoveredBritain.com.*

Two good books about access in the UK are *Holidays in Britain and Ireland* and *Accessible Britain 2000/01. Holidays in Britain and Ireland* is published annually by the Royal Association for Disability and Rehabilitation (RADAR) and includes access information on lodgings and attractions in the UK and Republic of Ireland. Each lodging listing contains important access details such as door widths, and the availability of ground floor bedrooms, lifts (elevators) and adapted bathroom facilities. The guide also contains information on transportation and voluntary and commercial organizations throughout the country.

Accessible Britain 2000/01 is published by the English Tourism Council in conjunction with Holiday Care, and contains information on accessible attractions and accommodations throughout the UK. All accommodations are rated according to the Tourism For All national access scheme. The Information contained in the guide is based on information submitted to the English Tourism Board about inspected establishments. The publication also highlights accessible attractions in each area. Contact Holiday Care to order your copy.

Down on the Continent, access standards and laws vary from country to country; however there are some things that apply across the board. At the top of the access list is terminology; more specifically the difference between an adapted room and an accessible room.

An accessible room is a room which presents no obstacles to moving about in a wheelchair, but offers no specific amenities. An adapted room is a room in which the bathroom, shower and toilets are adapted to comply with access standards. So, if you need a roll-in shower or a raised toilet, don't ask for an accessible room. Roll-in showers are quite common throughout Europe, but you do need to specify your needs. They are sometimes called "level entry" or "no rim" showers. Also remember, in Europe the first floor is not at street level. If you want a room at street level, ask for a room on the ground floor.

There is also a different key scheme for accessible public toilets in continental Europe. The Euro Key scheme is administered by CBF, a German disability organization. In 1986 CBF started the Euro-key scheme in Germany, and today it has expanded to include many other European countries. The Euro-key is available for 25 DM, or you can get a guide book and a Euro-key for 30 DM from CBF.

And finally, here are a few European access resources. I've tried to limit my list to national disability organizations that freely provide access information. I've intentionally omitted any business or organization that sell tours or travel services. In France, the best access resource is CNRH, the French national disability organization. CNRH has free accessibility information on their website, and they also sell a print version of the guide. In Germany, Movado is the organization to contact. This German disability organization maintains a searchable database that includes detailed access information on lodgings, restaurants, shopping and other services in Berlin. And if your travels take you to Florence, Italy, contact Barrier Free Travel, an Italian non-profit organization founded by American Cornelia Danielson. Barrier Free Travel offers free access information on Florence and the surrounding area.

Down Under—With the passage of the Disability Discrimination Act (DDA) of 1992, access for people with disabilities in Australia has greatly improved in recent years. The DDA states that it is unlawful for providers of goods, services, and facilities to discriminate against a person with a disability. This includes public accommodations such as restaurants, lodgings, transportation and entertainment venues. The Human

Rights and Equal Opportunity Commission (HREOC) is the enforcement authority of the DDA.

In practice, Australia offers good access to lodging and most tourist facilities. The big exception is public transportation. In fact, this exception gained international attention in October 2000, during the run of the Sydney Paralympic Games. The Paralympic Games created the biggest demand for accessible transportation ever experienced in Australia, and the Olympic Roads and Transport Authority (ORTA) was responsible for coordinating that transportation. How'd they do? Well, according to many disability rights advocates, "not very well."

The situation came to a head in June 2000, when ORTA applied to the Australian HREOC for a temporary exemption from the DDA. The rationale behind the application was that since there were not enough accessible buses in New South Wales to serve the expected Olympic crowds, ORTA would have to procure them from public and private bus operators throughout the country. ORTA sought to protect these cooperating operators from any liability which might arise from the temporary transfer of their accessible buses to Olympic and Paralympic related services.

Disability advocates were outraged at ORTA's request, but in the end the exemption was approved by the HREOC. Buses were pulled from other areas, and sent to Sydney for the Olympics and Paralympics. Of course, many residents went without accessible transportation during that time. The reason? Well, accessible transportation is still in it's infancy in Australia, and there just aren't enough buses to go around. For many years, disability advocates have been pushing for the development of standards for accessible public transportation in Australia. Unfortunately it just hasn't happened yet. Hopefully this incident will serve to remind the powers that be, about the importance of accessible public transportation.

On the positive side, Australia does have some very unique access resources. At the top of the list is NICAN, a national database which contains access information on accommodations, tourist attractions and recreational facilities throughout Australia. NICAN maintains over 4,500 disability related resources in their database. Access information is available free from NICAN by phone, fax, e-mail or in person. You can also search the NICAN database on-line at *www.nican.com.au.*

Another great Australian innovation is the mobility map. These city maps depict the access features of local business districts, and are usually available through city tourism departments. The maps include information on accessible routes, telephones, toilets, and parking. They also include local landmarks, tourist attractions and street gradients. The city of Melbourne publishes an excellent mobility map, which is also available on-line at *www.accessmelbourne.vic.gov.au.* I'd love to see this concept catch on in other countries, but so far Australia is the only place that has really developed this resource.

Two excellent books about accessible travel in Australia are *Easy Access Australia* and *The Wheelie's Handbook of Australia*. First published in 1995, *Easy Access Australia* is packed full of helpful accessibility information. Author Bruce Cameron lists the major tourist attractions and hotels in each section. The second edition, published in 2000, contains approximately 600 accommodations, with 300 bathroom floorplans. Information on accessible transportation is also included, along with lots of contact information, phone numbers and maps. Very nicely done!! *The Wheelie's Handbook of Australia*, authored by Colin James, contains hard-to-find access details on over 500 accessible accommodations throughout Australia. Properties are listed by city and divided by geographic region. Each listing contains a detailed description of the property, plus access features, contact information and (sometimes) unexpected extras. Both books are available directly from the authors.

And finally, New Zealand is not without it's share of access resources. Although a variety of disability and rehabilitation organizations offer bits and pieces of access information, the most comprehensive New Zealand resource is Enable Tourism New Zealand. This handy service provides updated access information on New Zealand's lodging, transportation and tourist attractions. Limited access information is available on the Enable Tourism New Zealand website at *www.mysite.xtra.co.nz/~enabletour*; while more detailed and personalized information is available upon request.

Electricity and Converters—Access standards aren't the only differences you'll encounter when you travel outside of the US. One difference of major importance to many wheelers is the electrical voltage outside of North America. In short, if you travel with a rechargeable battery, you need to learn how to safely recharge your battery while you're on foreign soil. Of course, it goes without saying that you also need to formulate a contingency plan; just in case something goes wrong.

The United States, Canada and most countries in the Western hemisphere operate on 110 volt electricity. Most other countries operate on 220 volt electricity. Additionally, some countries also have plug configurations that are different from those in the US. So, you need two things to safely charge your battery overseas. First you need a converter or transformer; to safely convert the foreign electricity. Additionally, you may also need an adapter so that your US style plug will fit in the foreign socket. What happens if you don't use a converter? Quite simply, you will fry your battery charger. Although it sounds pretty basic, many people get into trouble because they don't think before they plug in their equipment.

For example, some countries have that familiar two prong outlet found across the US; however, they also operate on 220 voltage. The plug fits in the socket nicely, but if you don't also use a converter you'll fry your charger. Remember, the only thing an adapter does is change the shape of the plug. It does nothing to convert the electricity. Many people get into trouble when they only use an adapter. Just because the plug fits into the socket, doesn't mean that it's safe to plug in your equipment. Before you plug in your battery charger, always ask yourself, "Do I need a converter?" Don't plug in your equipment until you know the definitive answer. Nothing ruins a vacation faster than a fried battery charger.

What kind of a converter do you need? Well the first thing you need to do is to find out the voltage, amperage, and wattage of your battery charger. This information is usually written on your charger, but if you can't find it, consult your owner's manual. If you still can't find this information, write down the make and model of your wheelchair, call the manufacturer and ask for the technical support department. Says scooter-user Carol Randall, "Of all the calls I've made, I have found these technical support people to be the most knowledgeable and helpful. They can usually tell you exactly what you will need, and where you can get it." It's a good idea to consult your wheelchair manufacturer in this situation, as they are the experts on your particular wheelchair, and they will recommend the most appropriate converter for your needs.

You'll probably also need also some adapters to go along with your converter. Which adapters should you buy? Well, that depends on where you plan to travel. A good information resource for adapters is Magellan's, a mail order catalogue for travel supplies. They have a good table on adapters and lots of valuable information on their website and in their print catalogue. Additionally they will answer individual questions about specific needs. Of course they also carry just about every adapter known to man.

If you travel a lot, or you just don't want to bother with thinking about converters and electricity, you might want to consider buying a universal battery charger. They are available through a variety of companies, and can be installed on your wheelchair. Check with your wheelchair manufacturer to see what model will work best for you. The advantage to a universal charger is that you don't have to carry a special converter in order to use electricity in a foreign country. It's the safest way to proceed, however most universal chargers run over $250. You may still need some adapters to use with your universal charger, depending on your destination. A universal charger is a good idea if you plan to travel overseas frequently.

What do you do if, in spite of all your efforts, you do fry your battery charger? It happens to the best of us, including experienced travelers like Carol Randall; so you should at least think about a contingency plan. Fortunately, Carol's quick thinking provided her a creative solution that saved her trip. Says Carol of her experience, "After I fried my charger in London, I headed over to the local automotive supply store and bought an inexpensive 12-volt, low output battery charger for $20. The drawback was that we had to disconnect the batteries and it would only charge one battery at a time. This meant we had to get up once during the night to change the charger; but it did work, and it saved the trip." Other helpful suggestions include carrying a photo of a battery charger and the words "battery charger" written in the local language. These items will help you if you need to go in search of a battery charger in a country where you don't speak the language.

Other Concerns—Medical issues are a concern no matter where you travel, but they take on an added importance when you travel outside of the US. While your medical insurance will most likely cover you throughout the US, it may not cover you in a foreign country. Check with your insurance company before you depart. If your insurance does cover you outside of the US, be sure and carry the appropriate medical cards and insurance forms. Find out how to file an overseas claim. Although nobody plans to seek medical care while on a vacation, accidents do happen. The best strategy is to be prepared.

You'll also want to find out if your destination country has some sort of national health care program that also covers travelers. Some countries do, and they provide free emergency medical care to anyone, even visitors. It pays to ask a few questions, as it may prevent you from buying unneeded medical insurance. If you don't have any other coverage, you may want to buy some travel medical or health insurance that will cover you overseas. Some travel agents sell this, but it's really best to check with your insurance agent. After all they are the experts about insurance issues. Make sure that any travel insurance you purchase doesn't exclude pre-existing conditions.

One of the biggest costs of a medical emergency overseas, is the cost of medical evacuation. If you should have an accident and can't fly home on a regular airline, you'll need to hire an air ambulance. Some types of insurance already cover this. For example, when I upgraded my auto club membership to AAA Plus, I got the added benefit of $25,000 of emergency medical transportation coverage. It's incredibly economical and it covers me for the entire year, no matter where I travel. Check with your insurance company about travel insurance plans. They are affordable and some even include trip cancellation and accidental death coverage. Again, it's very important to make sure that your policy does not exclude pre-existing medical conditions. Additionally, it's usually more economical to buy a policy that covers you year round; as opposed to a short term policy that only covers you for one trip.

Of course many travel agents also sell all sorts of trip cancellation and travel insurance. Some travel agents even make you sign a form which states you declined to purchase coverage from them. They are not doing this to scare you, but rather to protect themselves from liability should something happen to you. They also like everybody to have travel insurance, because they don't want unhappy clients; and when clients have to cancel a trip and don't get their money back, they are unhappy. Although most travel agents are reputable, it's best to see your own insurance agent regarding any travel insurance issues. Again, they are the experts in all insurance matters.

Of course, always take a copy of all your prescriptions with you when you travel. Carry them in your carry-on baggage. Some people also take a brief medical history with them, in case they have a medical emergency and are unable to communicate. You might also want to check into getting a Medic Alert bracelet if you have a special medical condition or unique medical needs. And finally, if you are going to a foreign country, learn a few words of the language. At the top of the list is "wheelchair". If you can't manage the pronunciation, then just write it down and carry with you. It may come in quite handy.

Where To Begin—Where do you begin your research for your overseas trip? Well, the first rule of thumb is to try and deal directly with organizations or people in your destination country. Although many people in the US are experienced with overseas travel, the locals have the most updated and accurate information.

Wherever you travel, there will most likely be some set of rules governing accessibility, and the best way to find out about these is through a national disability organization. Disabled Peoples' International, an international cross disability network, has a good list of worldwide disability organizations on their website at *www.dpi.org*.

Another good resource are the foreign counterparts of US disability organizations. For example, if your travels take you to the UK, you might want to check out the MS Society of the UK. The internet is a great tool for this type of research. Post notices in travel forums and on disability focused websites, The goal is to find a local contact. Generally speaking if you ask enough people, sooner or later you will find a good contact.

And finally, don't forget about foreign tourist bureaus. Some offices now have access information and some even publish access guides. It never hurts to ask, and they may be able to give you a local contact.

11 | The Travel Agent

Friend or Foe?

You've finally decided that it's time for a vacation; so what's the first thing you need to do? Well, according to most other books about accessible travel, you need to "Find a good travel agent." To be honest, that's pretty useless advice. After all, nobody wants to find a "bad" travel agent.

Sarcasm aside, there are several things you need to understand before you go in search of that perfect travel agent. First, you need to determine if you even need a travel agent; and to do this, you need to understand how travel agents work and what they can and can't do for their clients. In the long run this will also help you work more effectively with your agent. Of course you also need to know how to find a travel agent that best suits your needs. To do this, you need to learn a little bit about the industry, so you know how to recognize a "good" travel agent. Additionally you need to be able to recognize a bad travel agent, along with some of the pitfalls and scams that seem to proliferate in this industry. As with everything else, it's definitely a case of "buyer-beware".

Travel Agent 101—Travel agents work in a variety of ways, but in the simplest form they book travel for clients and receive commissions from suppliers (cruise lines, hotels, airlines, tour companies). The products they offer are dependent upon their business relationships and commission arrangements with the suppliers. So in theory, two different travel agents could work with a number of different suppliers, and as a result offer their clients different travel options. I say "in theory", because it doesn't always work that way. In practice, many "mainstream" travel agents only work with the suppliers that pay the highest commissions. On the other hand, there are a limited number of travel agents that specialize in accessible travel. By that I mean the majority of their clients require accessible travel arrangements. There are only a limited number of suppliers that provide accessible services, so the agents that (really) specialize in accessible travel know these providers. The big problem is finding these specialists. More on that later.

The truth is that many small "accessible" tour operators simply cannot afford to pay out commissions. So, these small guys are effectively left out of the booking loop. Some travel agents won't work with suppliers who do not pay commissions. It's just simple economics. Travel agents and tour operators both need to make money. Travel agents can't afford to work for free, so they have to work with suppliers that can pay commissions. Small tour operators need to make a living, so most can't afford to pay out commissions. Sometimes it's a vicious circle.

But it's not just the small tour operators that don't pay commissions to travel agents. Years ago, most airlines paid out hefty commissions, but over the years those commissions have dwindled. Today it's hard for many travel agents to even pay for their reservation software with the meager commissions offered by most airlines. The result is that some agents no longer work with "air only" clients, while others now charge a minimal processing fee for domestic air tickets. Generally speaking, travel agents still receive a decent commission on international airline tickets, so most are still willing to offer this service.

As a result of dwindling commissions, many travel agents found different ways to address the travel market. The professional organizations encouraged travel agents to find profitable niche markets, such as accessible travel. Many travel agents became "accessible travel specialists" overnight. I say this sarcastically because, officially, there is no such thing as a certified "accessible travel specialist". Of course you can say whatever you want to on your own business cards and in your own promotional literature. On the other hand, there are a number of genuine accessible travel specialists out there; and most of these experienced agents have served this niche market long before it was ever fashionable. But, with so many Johnny-come-latelys popping up, sometimes it is hard to find the real accessible travel experts.

Then there are the destination specialists and itinerary planners. These are highly trained experts, and I encourage you to actively seek them out. Destination specialists focus on a particular destination and they are experts about everything related to that destination. Many of these destination specialists are also knowledgeable about access. Some destination specialists also do itinerary planning. Itinerary planners charge their clients for their services. Sometimes they also get commissions from suppliers, but these travel agents don't exclusively work only with suppliers that pay out commissions. These travel professionals are worth their weight in gold; however be on the lookout for impostors. Nobody can be a destination specialist for all areas of the world, so be wary of any travel agent who makes that claim.

In truth, I know a lot of good travel agents; in fact some of my best friends are travel agents. Unfortunately I've also heard horror stories about the bad travel agents, so I know they are out there. Good travel agents work hard for their money, and offer their clients valuable first hand knowledge about products, services and destinations. The bad ones? They can ruin your trip and make you swear off travel forever.

Do You Need One?—Do you need a travel agent? There's not a blanket answer to that question. In truth it depends on many factors, including your travel needs and your own personality type. This book gives you the tools to cut out the middleman and in a sense, "be your own travel agent". But do you really want to do that? Some people do and some people don't.

Many people work with travel agents because they want somebody else to take care of all the details. So, if you don't want to deal with the hundreds of minor details that can pop up before, during and after your trip, then by all means delegate the task to a competent travel agent. But, planning and knowledge are two different things; so remember, just because you delegate the trip planning task to a travel agent, doesn't mean you shouldn't also educate yourself about the logistics of accessible travel and the accessibility of your destination. Regardless of who makes your travel arrangements, you still need to know your rights and understand the process. Why? Because the real proof of a genuine accessible travel specialist lies with their knowledge about the rules, regulations and realities of accessible travel; and the only way to judge that is to become an expert yourself.

As I pointed out earlier, many travel agents don't want to bother with domestic air only tickets because it's simply not profitable; so if you are just looking for the lowest fare to Cincinnati, then it's usually best to bypass the travel agent. Let's face it, sometimes the logistics of accessible travel are time intensive, and most agents just can't afford to spend this time with clients pro bono. Like everybody else, they need to be paid for their time, and if the airlines won't pay them; well, they simply can't afford to work for free. Nobody can.

On the other hand, travel agents can be quite helpful with international travel, package tours, cruise travel or group tours. These are pretty competitive markets, so make sure your agent is well versed in the finer aspects of accessible travel. For example, don't just use any cruise travel agent; use one that can tell you about the accessibility of the ports. Additionally, don't feel you are married to one agent forever; as different agents have different specialties. One agent may be a great cruise agent but know very little about land tours in the UK. Again, nobody can be an expert at everything, so choose an expert that works best for your particular trip.

Giving equal time to travel agents, some travel agents do go above and beyond the call of duty for regular clients. As one travel agent confides, "I've done some ridiculously time consuming things for long term clients, just as favors because they've used me for years." Truthfully, the best reason to work with any travel agent is to take advantage of their destination and access knowledge. A good travel agent is a very valuable resource.

The Search—The search for a travel agent begins much the same way as the search for any other professional. The best strategy is gather a list of potential candidates and then interview them over the phone. Where do you find the candidates? Well, personal referrals are great, so ask your friends and family if they know of any good travel agents. Be sure and specify that your definition of a good travel agent is one that is well educated about accessible travel.

Scan through national disability magazines, search the internet, ask people in your support group, and look for advertisements in the yellow pages. Learn to read between the lines of advertisements though. I recently spied an advertisement in a national disability magazine that didn't even list a phone number, company name, or address. The only contact information for this advertisement that touted "accessible tours of Ireland", was an e-mail contact. After a little investigation I learned that this individual was ill equipped to organize accessible tours, as he wasn't even aware of the accessible transportation situation in Ireland. The big tip off should have been the lack of contact information. Skip over any advertisement that just doesn't have a professional look.

Soon your list of candidates will grow and you'll be ready to begin the interview process. Before you pick up the phone, remember that it's important to ask all the candidates the same questions. Try to talk to at least five candidates. Even if you absolutely love the first candidate, continue to call everybody on your list. You never know, you may just find somebody you love even more. Feel free to eliminate anybody you just don't like; even if they seem to have the appropriate professional qualifications. Go with your gut feeling. This is a personal service and you need to feel comfortable with your travel agent. You don't have to become best friends, but you can't really work effectively with somebody who you just don't like.

Be sure and inquire about what kind of training the agent has, and how long they have worked with accessible travel. Nobody is born with this knowledge, so remember we all have to learn it at some time in life. Don't rule out "real life" experience either. An agent may be very experienced in accessible travel because they have a disability. This type of "real life" experience is invaluable, however by itself it is not enough. The agent also has to be familiar with the travel industry. Ask about their professional qualifications. If they have a lot of initials after their name, ask what they mean, and how they got them.

It's also a good idea to throw in a test question, just to make sure they have the requisite knowledge about accessible travel. Now, I'm not saying you should cross examine and badger each candidate, but do ask at least one question that tests their accessible travel expertise.

If you have a specific destination in mind, ask about their expertise on that destination. Ask them what percentage of clients they book to that destination, and ask them when they last visited that destination.

Most importantly, ask them if they have experience dealing with clients with "your disability". Ask for references, and call up those references and inquire about their travel experiences. Now, to be honest you may run into some travel agents who won't give you references.

Some travel agents are gun-shy because of their past experiences with providing references. Says one long time travel agent, "I used to give out references (with my clients' permission), until I had a bad experience. A few years ago a lady requested references and then she badgered the heck out my client. She kept calling her up and just wanted to chit-chat and be her best friend. My client didn't want anything to do with her, and she had a hard time getting rid of her. I don't give out references any more. I just can't risk another experience like that one."

So, I wouldn't disqualify a potential candidate just because they won't provide you with references; as sometimes there is a very good reason behind this decision. You'll just have to rely on your own judgment in this matter; however if the travel agent doesn't have the time to answer your questions, then move on. Answering a few personal questions is easy, compared to the intricacies of researching and arranging accessible travel.

Some Red Flags—Once you've completed the interview process, how do you evaluate the answers and pick the best travel agent? Well, the personality factor will serve to screen out some candidates. In fact you will probably run across a few agents that you just don't like. They are easy to scratch off the list. But what about the rest? Your final decision should be based on the candidates' destination and access knowledge; but, there are also a few responses that should throw up a red flag.

Be wary when somebody tells you they are a "certified" accessible travel expert. There's nothing wrong with somebody saying they have experience in this specialty, but as I pointed out earlier, there is no official "certification" training or process. Ask what exactly they mean, and how much training (if any) they have. Ask them how long they have been in the industry and how long they have been working with accessible travel. Some people call themselves experts after an afternoon training seminar.

Watch out for candidates who tout their membership in a professional organization as their primary qualification as an accessible travel specialist. Ask about the organization's membership requirements. There are a large number of professional organizations for travel agents; and while some have rigid membership criteria, others merely require members to write out an annual check.

A red flag should go up if a candidate guarantees you something that is simply not within his power. For example, if someone guarantees you bulkhead seats, "no matter what", this only serves to illustrate their own ignorance about the Air Carriers Access Act. Additionally, be wary of any agent that guarantees you a problem-free trip. Travel is unpredictable, and nobody knows when problems will arise.

Stay away from anybody that uses that dreaded h-word. It's all right to use this word to describe horses and golfers, but not to describe people with disabilities. It shows a general lack of knowledge and sensitivity about the market; and that lack of knowledge usually doesn't stop at terminology. Most likely this person is also lacking in essential knowledge about the logistics of accessible travel.

Some agencies advertise that they are "owned and operated by a person with a disability". Although there's nothing really wrong with stating that fact, be wary if that in itself is the agent's only qualification. Of course you should also ask what their disability is, if they make it a point to include this fact in their advertisements. Look for somebody who is experienced and knowledgeable about your disability. For example, just because a person is blind, doesn't mean he has a good working knowledge about wheelchair-travel.

Watch out for agents that use broad generalizations, such as "everything is accessible." This indicates a general lack of knowledge on the subject.

Finally, be wary of travel agents who don't travel. If they don't travel ask them why (sometimes there is a good reason); and then ask them what they do to keep up with the industry. The ideal agent should have also traveled to your destination recently; however this isn't always possible. Additionally, be wary of travel agents who "always" travel. Some people get into the travel business just so they can write off their own travel expenses.

Although there's nothing wrong with that per se, your travel agent should be available to answer your questions and deal with problems as they arise; and that's just not possible if they are always on the road.

Buyer Beware!—There are a few things that you need to be extra cautious about, when searching for a travel agent. I hate to blatantly call them scams, however they deserve more attention than the red flag items. By far the worst one of these items is the "you too can be a travel agent" scam. And yes, I do classify this one as a scam.

Also known as a card mill, this scam is incredibly damaging to consumers and professionals alike. Many people unknowingly fall prey to it even if they aren't in the market for a job. In fact, the biggest market for card mill operators is people who like to travel, not just people who need a job. This scam works in a variety of ways, and indeed some are quite slick. Typically the con man tries to convince you that it's in your best interest to become a travel agent, because you can save money on your own travel. He'll also tell you about how you can book travel for your friends and family, and make big bucks with little or no effort. And then he'll rave about the free and discounted travel you can receive as a official card carrying travel agent. What's he selling? Not much, usually just a card saying you are a travel agent and maybe a manual of some sort. Both items are pretty worthless.

Card mills can present themselves in a variety of ways, including self employment opportunities. This is perhaps the most straightforward approach, as at least you know what they are selling. Other approaches aren't so straightforward and can include advertisements that read "travel for free" or "save big money on travel". Additionally, card mill operators are taking full advantage of the underemployment in the disabled community by actively soliciting people with disabilities with the enticing promise of a turn-key home based business that makes big bucks. Be careful when somebody offers you something that sounds too good to be true. The truth is, real travel agents work very hard for their money, and most have had some kind of hands-on training. It's not easy work, and many travel agents take years to turn a profit and establish their business. As for the travel agent discounts and fam trips; well travel suppliers are familiar with card mills too, so "card mill travel agents" are routinely screened out of most offerings.

So, be very wary of anybody who tries to sell you a home based travel business; as they could in fact be a card mill operator. Unfortunately, many people fall for this scam, and as a result there are a number of card mill travel agents out there. Worse yet, some of these untrained travel agents specialize in accessible travel. All the more reason to carefully screen your travel agent candidates!

Another thing to be on the lookout for are travel agents or tour operators that operate as non-profit agencies. This practice isn't something that I actually classify as a scam, but it can be pretty misleading. True, there are some legitimate non-profit organizations that do offer accessible trips and tours; however some businesses operate as non-profits in name only. It's merely an accounting method for some. They still make money and take a salary. There's really nothing wrong with that, unless they imply otherwise.

So if your tour operator or travel agent claims non-profit status, ask about the services they provide for the community. If the best they can come up with is, "We negotiate good deals on travel," then you may be dealing with a non-profit in name only. Remember, operating a non-profit organization doesn't necessarily guarantee altruistic motives. To some, it's just a marketing tool. Ask a lot of questions whenever a travel agency or tour operator touts their non-profit status.

And finally, be very wary if something just doesn't sound right. Recently a travel agent told me this horrifying story. A man called her after he had booked a group tour to Europe with another travel agent. The man used a power wheelchair and required assistance to transfer. He was feeling a little anxious about his upcoming tour because no arrangements for accessible transportation or lodging had been mentioned. He confronted his travel agent with his fears and she told him, "Don't worry, all of Europe is completely accessible". This should have sent up a big red warning flag!! Fortunately the second travel agent told the man the truth. So ask around, do your research and if something just doesn't sound right, use your common sense and investigate further. And if somebody tells you, "All of Europe is completely accessible," run (or roll) as fast as you can in the opposite direction!!

Travel Agent Etiquette—Choosing a travel agent is only half of the battle. Now that you understand how the travel industry works, you can use this knowledge to work more effectively with your travel agent. Here are a few pointers to help you along the way.

First and foremost, don't waste a travel agent's time. For example, don't call up a travel agent and just ask for a list of accessible hotels. Remember what travel agents do. They are not a public information resource. They book trips and use their expertise for their clients. Says one travel agent, "Last week one caller took up about three hours of our time. She wanted detailed information on accessible ships, accessible ports, and ports where her service dog could come ashore. She asked for multiple rates on different ships and cabins. Then her traveling companion decided she felt more comfortable booking locally, so she took all the information she gleaned from us and booked with another travel agent. I now understand why so many specialists require non-refundable goodwill deposits."

Of course if your travel agent is making travel arrangements for you, then it's perfectly acceptable to ask for a choice of hotels in a particular city; but don't just call up any agent, ask for the information and make the arrangements yourself. If you want to make your own travel arrangements, find another information source.

Be well prepared when you first contact your travel agent. Have some idea of where you want to go, when you want to go and how long you want to stay. Have a general idea about your travel budget. It's all right to go to your travel agent with a few choices, and ask for their opinion; but don't just walk in and expect them to find the right trip for you. Do some advance research and make a list of destinations that interest you, and then inquire about their suitability when you talk with your travel agent.

Be honest with your travel agent (and yourself) about your disability. It won't benefit anybody if you hide important information; in fact anything short of full disclosure can be disastrous. Consider the plight of Judy B., who ended up stranded at Denver International Airport, because of a failure to disclose. Judy, a 52 year old woman with MS, was no longer able to travel independently due to progressive cognitive difficulties. Unfortunately, when Judy's daughter made the travel arrangements she neglected to mention her mom's cognitive difficulties to the travel agent. She only said that her mom needed some wheelchair assistance. After Judy landed in Denver, she got confused and didn't know where she was. She missed her connecting flight to Bismark. Of course she assured everybody she was all right, and was just waiting for her daughter. Finally, security stepped in and came to Judy's aid. Unfortunately by this time Judy's pants were soaked with urine, and her daughter was worried sick in Bismark. The whole situation could have been easily avoided with a little honesty.

Now, I'm not saying that you need to give out a complete medical history; but don't hide important facts. For example, if you can't transfer independently, then you need to be honest with your travel agent about this fact. It won't prevent you from going on a trip; but it will help your travel agent plan a trip that is appropriate for you. Most likely your travel agent will have a questionnaire for you to complete. Try to answer all the questions as completely as possible; however if a particular question makes you feel uncomfortable, do talk this over with your travel agent. Ask why they need to know that information.

Remember, "I don't know," is sometimes an acceptable answer; in fact it's better than a wrong answer or a guess. Nobody knows all the answers, but a good travel agent has the resources to find them. Allow your travel agent time to research your question, and be glad you have a travel agent who is willing to do the research. However, if your travel agent continually answers "I don't know" to your questions and is unwilling to do the research, then perhaps you need to look elsewhere.

Don't call your travel agent for daily updates about your travel arrangements. Remember, you are not their only client. Admittedly you will have questions, so write them down and consolidate them into one phone call. Now, I'm not saying don't ever call your travel agent. For example, if your agent promised to call you back on a certain date, and that time has passed, then by all means pick up the phone. Calling for daily updates only tends to frustrate travel agents, as time is a very important commodity to them. Give them a fair chance to do their job. If you don't trust your travel agent to make the appropriate arrangements, then perhaps it's time to find somebody that you do trust.

Don't blame your travel agent because your "dream destination" is not accessible. Instead, work with your agent to find a suitable alternative. The truth is, some countries are just not very accessible, and it will take more than your travel agent to change that fact. You should expect an honest evaluation about access from your travel agent, but don't blame your agent if it's not exactly what you want to hear. In other words, don't shoot the messenger!

If your travel agent is working on a package tour or cruise for you, do remember to inquire about the access of all facets of your trip. This includes transportation, transfers, accommodations and day trips. For cruises, it's very important to ask about the accessibility of shore excursions. Outside the US there are few accessible shore excursions, so work with your travel agent to arrange your own accessible shore excursions.

Finally, remember it's standard practice for travel agents to ask for a deposit. If they are making independent travel arrangements for you, the deposit will be deducted from your final bill. If you cancel, then they will most likely retain the deposit in order to cover fax and phone costs. If you're a booking a package tour or cruise, the deposit requirements are set by the supplier. Make sure you have a good understanding of the deposit agreement. Don't be afraid to ask your travel agent for clarification, before you write out that check.

The Way It Should Be—Ideally, all travel agents should have a working knowledge of accessible travel. But, what if your long-time travel agent doesn't have this knowledge? This question comes up often, from people who are recently injured or newly disabled and who want to work with the same travel agent they have been using for the past 20 years. What do you do in this case?

Well, if your travel agent seems willing to learn, and you feel comfortable dealing with her, then I say give it a try. But, don't expect perfection overnight. Your agent will be learning something new, and it may take a while for her to learn all the ins and outs of accessible travel. It is, as you know, an extremely complex subject. The advantage to working with your present agent is that you most likely feel comfortable working with her, as you have developed a relationship over the years. But remember, it will be incumbent upon you to tell your agent of your needs, especially since she is not used to working with clients with disabilities.

In truth, everybody has their own definition of the "perfect society". My Utopia comes equipped with all the standard features (universal health care, courteous cab drivers and an unlimited supply of chocolate); but it also has an few added options. In my Utopia, all travel agents (not just the specialists) have a good working knowledge of accessible travel and disability issues.

Furthermore, every travel agent is able to book accessible tours, rooms and transportation for anybody that happens to walk or roll into their office. That's just the way it should be!

But, as you may well know, that's not exactly the way things work today. Perhaps someday soon, all travel agents will have a working knowledge of accessible travel. Until then, take care when selecting your travel agent, as your research, time and effort will pay off in the long run.

12 | Shopping The Net

The Truth About On-Line Booking

Nobody is ambivalent about the internet. Some folks claim it's the greatest thing since sliced bread, while others blame it for the downfall of modern society. Regardless of your feelings about the internet, it's a great tool for travel junkies. But, is on-line booking a realistic option for wheelers? The answer is a "conditional" yes. In reality there isn't a "one click" method; but you can use the internet to save money and to insure appropriate access. What's the best way to do this? Well, there's not a blanket answer to that question. In truth it depends on what type of travel arrangements you are booking, as the "best method" varies drastically from reserving a hotel room to making an airline reservation.

Reserving A Room—Theoretically, booking a hotel room on-line should be a fairly easy process. In practice however, it doesn't quite work that way. This is especially true when you throw access issues into the equation. Unfortunately there are a few problems inherent in the hotel industry that just makes it difficult to book an accessible room on-line. Not impossible, just difficult.

There are two basic roadblocks to booking an accessible room on-line. First off, we go back to that age old problem of defining access. Most hotel websites, travel portals, and consolidators don't list the specific access features of their accessible rooms. At best, they define their rooms as being "accessible" or "ADA compliant". But what access features do these rooms have? Sometimes it's hard to tell. Does the room you're booking have a roll-in shower? Is it on the ground floor? How wide is the bathroom door? How high is the toilet? Unfortunately these important details are not listed on most websites. So, it does require a bit of research (and sometimes a few phone calls) to find out what features are included in an accessible room at a particular property. And of course the criteria can change from property to property. The first rule of on-line booking is to always contact the property directly for the most accurate access information.

Second, it's hard to determine if a property will guarantee or "block" their accessible rooms, just by looking at their website. Is this important? You bet your bottom dollar. It's useless to reserve an accessible room, if it's not there for you when you arrive. Contact the hotel directly regarding their policy on this matter, and don't do business with hotels that won't block their accessible rooms.

Although these roadblocks make it harder to book an accessible room on-line, they don't make it impossible. There are three main ways to book a hotel room on-line; by using either a hotel consolidator, a professional interface or the hotel's own website. Although these methods each have different advantages and disadvantages, it's a good idea to keep the basic roadblocks in mind while using any on-line booking system. That way, you'll be able to circumvent the inherent problems and book an accessible room that's right for you.

Hotel Consolidators—If you've ever searched for travel websites on the internet, you've probably visited your fair share of hotel consolidator websites. Hotel consolidators buy blocks of hotel rooms and resell them to the public at substantial discounts. You've probably also seen advertisements for hotel consolidators in the Sunday travel section, under a headline such as "save up to 50% on hotels." The good news is that you can indeed save anywhere from 20% to 50% off the rack rate by booking through a consolidator. The bad news is that it's virtually impossible to book an accessible room through a hotel consolidator. Worse yet, some consolidators are not very up front about their cancellation fees; so besides being impossible it can be downright costly. The best advice is to steer clear of hotel consolidator websites.

But, sometimes it's hard to recognize hotel consolidators, because many travel portals use them as booking engines. This is commonly referred to as an "affiliate relationship". Basically the travel portal uses the hotel consolidator interface and receives a commission for rooms booked from the portal website. The hotel consolidator interface is incorporated into the travel portal website, and sometimes it appears that you are booking directly with the travel portal, when in fact you are using a hotel consolidator.

It's pretty easy to recognize consolidators and their affiliates once you understand why it's impossible to use them for booking accessible rooms. First off, consolidators don't guarantee accessible rooms. You can state that you need an accessible room on the reservation form, but it's only treated as a request. In other words, you will get an accessible room if it's available when you arrive. To add insult to injury, this fact is usually only disclosed in the fine print. Additionally you must prepay your room charges when you book through a hotel consolidator; plus there's usually a substantial cancellation fee. So basically you pay in advance but you aren't guaranteed anything. If you get to the hotel and they don't have an accessible room for you, you're still on the hook for the cancellation fee. In short, it makes no difference why you cancel, even if the room doesn't suit your access needs.

One of the worst things about dealing with a consolidator is that you don't deal directly with the hotel. If you call the hotel to confirm your reservation they usually won't find a reservation under your name. The consolidators book big blocks of rooms, so your reservation is technically under the consolidator's name, until the last minute. So, it's impossible to communicate directly with the property about the specifics of your reservation, because as far as the property is concerned your reservation doesn't exist. Of course this makes it impossible to confirm the amenities of your accessible room. Are you starting to understand the problems associated with using a consolidator?

Unfortunately many people do fall prey to the evil hotel consolidator, including yours truly. Before I really learned about hotel consolidators I booked a room on-line at the Hotel Reservation Network (HRN). It seemed like a good deal at the time, even better than I could get by booking directly with the hotel. So I typed in my credit card number and hit "send". I figured that if I found a better deal, I could just cancel the reservation. I didn't see anything on the website about a cancellation fee. Of course HRN claims differently, but apparently the java script warning about the cancellation fee didn't work on my browser.

In any case, after I made my reservation I called the property directly to confirm that I had booked a non-smoking room. That's when I learned how consolidators work, as the hotel had no record of my reservation. I also found out that they didn't have any non-smoking rooms available on the days of my stay. So I decided to cancel. Well, I couldn't cancel with the hotel because they didn't have a record of my reservation. So I called HRN to cancel. Of course the reservation agent warned me about the $75 cancellation fee. I almost dropped the phone when I heard that, after all I was canceling several months in advance.

The cancellation fee seemed rather excessive to me, so I explained the situation to the reservation agent. It didn't matter. In fact, she told me "Even if you died we wouldn't waive the cancellation fee." That seemed like a rather drastic solution to me. The story does however have a happy ending, as once HRN found out that I was a travel writer they mysteriously agreed to waive the cancellation fee. But the bottom line is that I was let off the hook because of privilege, and the solution to my predicament effectively does nothing to change HRN's unreasonable cancellation policy.

So remember, never do business with hotel consolidators. In fact, never do business with any property or service that imposes an unreasonable cancellation fee. You really need the flexibility to cancel your reservation, especially when you're dealing with access issues.

The Professional Interface—The second way to book a hotel reservation on-line is through a professional interface; the same type of a reservation system that many travel agents use. Apollo and Sabre are two of the most popular interfaces, and they both have "lite" or "non-professional" versions. These "lite" versions are pretty easy to use, as they don't require any great technical expertise. You just need to know when and where you want to stay. The major advantage of using a professional interface is that you deal directly with the hotel. You request a reservation, the request goes to the hotel, and you get a confirmation number back; all within a matter of seconds. It's a pretty efficient system.

The downside to all this is that sometimes it's hard to tell a professional interface apart from a consolidator website, just by looking at the on-line booking form. Both forms ask you for the same information. There are however two big differences. One is that, aside from a no-show fee, you won't encounter a cancellation fee when using a professional interface. And two, when you use a professional interface, you don't have to pay the hotel charges in advance.

The professional interface can work well for booking an accessible room; however the success rate is directly dependent upon each individual property. In order to illustrate this point let's take a look at a popular on-line professional interface: the AAA of Northern California's travel reservation website, which uses the Apollo interface. On the AAA website members can search for available rooms based on date, location, hotel chain, price range and special preferences. One of the special preference items is an "accessible room".

So for example, a search for an accessible room in Baltimore on Aug. 2 will return a list of available accessible rooms for that date and location. You can then click on the hotel button to get a profile of the property, or click on the rate button to see the available rates for that day. So far so good; however your ability to book an accessible room depends upon the amount of access information that each individual property enters into their own reservation system. Some properties enter specific details about their accessible rooms, while others don't even separate the accessible rooms from the rest of their inventory. In some cases you can book an accessible room with a roll-in shower using the professional interface; however that's a best case scenario.

The plus side of this situation is that most of properties that take the time to enter access details about their inventory, are more conscientious about this market. So, in a way, you're not only booking an accessible room, but you're also screening for the most proactive properties. The down side is that sometimes it is a very long search. Still, the professional interface can be a very useful tool in the search for an accessible room. Of course you should always check with the hotel directly to confirm that they do in fact block their accessible rooms.

Hotel Websites—The best way to book an accessible room on-line is to make a reservation directly from the hotel's website. Of course, it's not as simple as it sounds; in fact there is a very specific procedure you should follow in order to make sure you get an accessible room.

The first step is to visit a number of hotel websites and check their rates for the dates of your visit. Pick the best rates and then call those properties directly to inquire about the specific features of their accessible rooms. Ask about each hotel's policy regarding blocking accessible rooms upon reservation. And, while you're on the phone go ahead and inquire about their rates. If they offer you a better rate than on the internet, and the room suits you needs, then by all means make a reservation. If not, then go back to the internet.

By now you've eliminated a number of properties; those that can't meet your access needs and those that won't block their rooms. Of the remaining properties, pick the one that has the best internet rate. Go to that property's website and book your reservation on-line. Make sure and specify your access needs. It never hurts to mention your access needs twice, so go ahead and also mention them in the comments section. Get a confirmation number and call the hotel directly to confirm you booking. If the reservation is not to your satisfaction, or you find out that the property cannot block an accessible room for you; then cancel the reservation. Of course, you'll now have to start the whole process all over again.

In truth, this whole process takes an awful lot of legwork. As I said earlier, it's not exactly a simple procedure. Indeed sometimes your long distance phone charges will far exceed that 5% internet discount. It helps to work with properties that have previously demonstrated a progressive attitude towards access issues. Unfortunately it's takes time and experience to recognize these properties. Still, some people find substantial savings on-line, and unfortunately many of these discounts are only available on-line. In the end you'll have to determine if the savings is really worth your time and effort. But if you do decide to use the internet to book your room, remember to use the hotel website. For now it's the safest way to book an accessible room on-line.

Finding A Flight—Admittedly, booking an "accessible" flight on-line is much easier than booking an accessible room on-line; quite simply because there are just fewer choices. But it does require some advance planning. Before you even begin to shop for airfares, you need to learn your rights under the Air Carriers Access Act (ACAA). Among other things, the ACAA mandates that a passenger with a disability cannot be denied boarding, solely because of their disability. In theory (and under AIR 21) the ACAA also covers foreign air carriers; however, in practice this legislation is difficult to enforce on foreign soil. Learn the law, and fly on US air carriers for the best access.

Even among US carriers, accessibility is still dependent on the aircraft, airline and airport you choose. Size does matter, so learn a little bit about the different types of commercial aircraft. Many of the ACAA regulations regarding aircraft accessibility and boarding are dependent upon aircraft size. The ACAA mandates level boarding whenever possible on all aircraft with 30 or more seats. In aircraft with fewer than 30 seats, level boarding is not required. Some airlines have aircraft diagrams available on their websites. You can also call the airlines directly to find out about the seating capacity and access features of specific aircraft types.

Seating is another important access issue. Wheelchair-users are not always guaranteed seating in bulkhead areas. Contact each airline directly to find out about their specific seating policies for wheelers. Some airlines will seat you in the bulkhead section, and some won't. Seating is addressed in the 1998 amendment to the ACAA, which was published in the March 4, 1998 issue of the *Federal Register*. Learn the rules, then contact airlines in advance to find out about their seating policies. Do business only with those airlines that can provide you appropriate seating.

Finally, do some research on your departure and arrival airports, as boarding options can be dependent on airport size. Not all airports have jetways to enable level boarding. Some regional airports board directly from the tarmac. Many airports have print access guides, and some even have access information posted on-line. Some airports have neither, so you'll just have to pick up the phone and call to find out about their accessibility.

Basically there are three major places to book flights on-line; on travel portals, auction websites or airline websites. However, it's only possible to make accessible flight arrangements in two of these places.

Travel Portals—Here's where things get confusing. Although it's a bad idea to book an accessible room through a travel portal, it's a great idea to use a travel portal to book an accessible flight. The reason is simple. Most travel portals utilize hotel consolidators for hotel reservations, but use a professional interface for airline reservations. So when you book a flight on a travel portal, you are most likely dealing directly with the airline.

After you've completed your initial research, search the travel portals for flights on US based airlines. Prices may vary from portal to portal, because each portal has strategic partnerships with different airlines. Some portals may only display prices from select airlines; while others may feature all airlines but only have competitive prices on a select few. Shop around for the best price, but keep your access needs in mind. You'll want to avoid small airplanes, regional airports and multi-legged flights. It's important to note that the best price for your access needs, may not necessarily be the cheapest price.

Book your flight when you find the best price. Airfares are somewhat volatile, so there's no guarantee that the same fare will be available next week. Most fares are based on load factors, and when fewer seats are available, the prices usually rise. Make note of your access requirements when you book your flight on-line. It's also a good idea to make note of any cancellation penalties. After you book your flight, call the airline and speak with the special services department to confirm your access requests. This is also a good time to request any special seating (if you qualify for it), or to request an on-board wheelchair. Additionally, remember to reconfirm all access arrangements 24 hours in advance.

Pig-In-A-Poke.Coms—Although the internet is a great tool for booking travel, there is one type of a travel website that people with disabilities should steer clear of; the "auction website" or the "name your price" website. These websites go by many different names and are promoted by scads of celebrities, but collectively I call them pig-in-a-poke.coms. Why? Well, because you buy merchandise (in this case airfares) sight unseen, without the benefit of important information that determines flight accessibility. It seems like a good idea at the time; however reality sets in when you arrive at the airport and find out you're booked on a turbo-prop that makes seven stops between Boise and Atlanta.

Pig-in-a-poke.coms all operate in much the same way. Basically you log on and either name you price or bid against other users for airline tickets and hotel rooms. Sounds pretty good, right? I mean, who wouldn't like to name their own price for an airline ticket? Well, the catch is that you can't chose your carrier, routing, aircraft or even the time of day you travel. In fact, you don't find out these details until after your bid is accepted and you pay for the ticket. And although this may be acceptable for travelers who don't have access needs, it's a big gamble for anybody who does. Unfortunately these websites are hyped heavily across cyberspace as being the "best places to find cheap airfares." Indeed they may be cheap, but many times the tickets are not useable by people with disabilities. The sad part is that most people don't find this out until it's too late.

The bottom line is, stay away from pig-in-a-poke.coms, as they don't offer choices of airlines, aircraft or routes; all of which are important factors in airline accessibility. Remember, a cheap airfare is no longer a bargain when you can't get on the airplane. And of course the tickets are non-refundable.

Airline Websites—The airline websites are good places to book air tickets on-line. In fact, it's a good idea to develop a relationship with one specific airline. It doesn't really matter which airline, and indeed the choice will be different for everybody. The advantages to working exclusively with one particular carrier are manyfold.

First off, you can collect frequent flyer miles and cash them in for free flights. Second, if you live near an airline's hub city, you'll be able to get more nonstop flights on that airline out of the hub city. This means fewer connections and fewer plane changes, which is great plus for wheelchair-users. And finally, if you travel on one particular airline, you'll be more familiar with their policies regarding people with disabilities. This includes everything from pre-boarding to seating. In short, you'll know what to expect.

You'll know immediately when something is wrong, and you'll be able to voice your complaint before it's too late. There are many benefits of one-carrier loyalty; however you may need to shop around until you find the airline that best suits your needs. Once you find that carrier, it pays to book on-line at the airline's website.

Most airline websites also offer special on-line deals or special promotions. If you book consistently with one airline, you can theoretically shop the sales. Of course this requires some advance planning, and familiarization with the airfares. After all, how do you know when you're getting a good deal on something unless you know the regular price? Plan your routes, check the fares and book on-line when the fares fall. Again, bear in mind that the best deal is not always the cheapest fare; the best deal should also include appropriate access for you.

Using an airline website to buy your ticket on-line just makes good sense, and (relatively speaking) it's a pretty simple procedure. Once you've found the right flight for you, purchase your ticket on the airline website. There is usually a drop down menu to indicate if "wheelchair assistance" is needed. Additionally, it doesn't hurt to make note of any special access requirements in the "comments" area. One word of caution, before you hit that "send" button, make sure you are familiar with the aircraft type used for the flight. Additionally, it doesn't hurt to have a look at the seating diagrams and even the cargo door dimensions. After you get a confirmation number, call the airline directly to make sure your access needs are properly noted; and to request special seating (if eligible) or an on-board wheelchair. Finally, make sure and call the airline to reconfirm all access arrangements, 24 hours prior to your flight.

The Solution—In truth there isn't one perfect solution for booking accessible travel arrangements on-line. Different people have different preferences and different needs. The best solution for many people may be a combination of the methods outlined above. It pays to be creative, so don't be afraid to customize a method that works best for you.

Learn your rights, plan your route, watch for airline sales and then book your best price on-line; or shop around for a travel agent to do it for you. After all, the internet isn't for everybody. The choice is yours. And as I said earlier, there isn't a one-click solution to on-line booking. Be wary of any website that claims otherwise. In reality, the internet is great tool for travelers; but remember, it's not the only tool.

13 | Accessible Recreation

A World Of Choices

For many people, recreation is an integral part of travel. In fact, for some people, it's the main reason for travel. People go to great lengths to enjoy their favorite recreational activities, at home and while on holiday. In the past, most recreational facilities only focused on able-bodied travelers, but today many facilities are now accessible to people with disabilities. Additionally, many companies, facilities and services are now using universal design to achieve barrier-free access. These welcome changes allow travelers with disabilities many new options for vacation-time recreational fun. Although there's literally a world of choices, here's a sampling of some accessible recreation possibilities.

Trails and Boardwalks—Let's start with the basics; accessible nature trails. They come in all shapes and sizes. It's great to be able to roll along a trail and get an up close and personal look at nature. Unfortunately, accessible trails are not the norm today, and you do have to search them out. However, the good news is that more developers are now incorporating the principles of universal design into trail construction whenever possible. Of course some folks have been doing this for years. Take the National Sports Center for the Disabled (NSCD) for example.

Founded in 1970, the NSCD is a non-profit organization based in Winter Park, Colorado. They provide a wide range of recreational opportunities for children and adults with disabilities; everything from skiing to sailing. They are truly the leaders in adaptive recreation in the United States. Among other things, they constructed the Bonfils Stanton Outdoor Center at their Winter Park location. This unique outdoor center includes a variety of accessible trails. It's the perfect venue for a bevy of accessible activities including camping, fishing, hiking and picnicking.

Accessible boardwalk at NSCD's Bonfils Stanton Outdoor Center in Winter Park, Colorado.

Variety is the keyword at Bonfils Stanton, especially when talking about accessible trails. Besides a 1.2 mile boardwalk they also have the Challenger Trail. This dirt trail has dips and rolls and grades from 2% to 6%, and was designed for those people who want to work up a sweat. There is no charge for admission or camping at Bonfils Stanton, but advance reservations are required for camping. The campground features raised tent platforms, and accessible restrooms, and is open from May 29 to September 30.

A little further south, in Kenosha Pass Colorado, Wilderness on Wheels (WOW) operates what they call a "Model Wilderness Access Facility". The WOW facility has an accessible boardwalk and cabins, plus camping and fishing facilities. All facilities were constructed by volunteers, and most of the materials were donated. The WOW boardwalk is eight feet wide and winds around a well stocked trout pond. This fishing pond is reserved for people with disabilities. There is a nearby stream for able-bodied fishermen. The boardwalk follows the contour of the land, and it's lined with willow trees and natural vegetation. Pack a picnic lunch and spend the day with nature at the WOW boardwalk, or plan to camp overnight.

The WOW facility offers two accessible options for overnight guests; campsites and a cabin. All campsites have raised tent platforms and one even has a covered dining area. The cabin is located on the ridge-top at the end of the boardwalk and it features all the comforts of home; stove refrigerator, beds and an accessible outhouse. There is no charge for admission or camping at the WOW boardwalk, but advance reservations are required. Members of WOW are eligible to rent the cabin for a minimal cost. The WOW facility is open form April to October.

Accessible campsite at WOW in Kenosha, Pass, Colorado.

Another accessible trail option are Rail Trails; trails that are built on abandoned rail corridors. There are more than 700 Rail trails across the US, and many are accessible. Most rail trails are flat or have a minimal grade so they are excellent for wheelchair-users and handcyclists. The Rails to Trails Conservancy in Washington DC has several guide books, plus on-line information about rail trail accessibility.

Additionally, you can search for accessible rail trails on the Trail Link Database at *www.traillink.com*. This searchable database contains information on Rails Trails throughout the US. You can search the database by state or by activity ("wheelchair access" is included as an activity). Each entry includes a description of the trail, including the length and surface composition, along with parking and trailhead information.

Many state, regional and local parks also have access information available. Of course this comes in a variety of forms. Some parks have access information on their websites and some even have access guides. And when all else fails, pick up the phone and ask to talk to the accessibility director, or somebody that is familiar with the access features of the park or facility. Remember, just because access information isn't prominently displayed doesn't mean that it doesn't exist; in fact sometimes it's hidden behind the counter, or in a forgotten corner of the office. Always remember to ask for access information!

National Parks—National Parks can also be good places for accessible recreation; although some parks are better than others. In truth, most parks have at least some facilities or services that are accessible, even if it's just a visitors center. Indeed there's a very wide variety of accessible trails and facilities in our national parks. Here's a sampling of what you will find.

Rocky Mountain National Park has some nicely-done accessible trails and accessible campsites. The nicest and newest accessible trail is the Coyote Valley Trail, located 5.4 miles from the west entrance to the park. It's made of hard packed dirt, and winds along the river and through a meadow. This interpretive trail is very accessible, and it's an excellent place to view wildlife. Other accessible trails are located at Bear Lake, Sprague Lake and Lily Lake.

In truth, trails are made accessible for different reasons. Over in Florida, the Everglades has a number of accessible boardwalks and a new accessible visitors center. These facilities were rebuilt to be accessible after they were destroyed by Hurricane Andrew. The boardwalk Anhinga Trail is one of the most accessible trails in the park. This half-mile boardwalk winds through sawgrass pines and Taylor Slough and is the home to a wealth of bird life. You'll see blue herons, white ibis and snowy egrets, along with the "namesake" anhingas. The anhingas (also called water turkeys) can be seen in abundance drying their colorful wings in the sun, or perched peacefully in trees along the trail. The Anhinga Trail is also an excellent place to get a close look at alligators.

Other accessible trails in the Everglades are the Pahayokee Trail, the Mahogany Hammock Trail and West Lake Trail. These boardwalk trails are all less than ¾ mile long, and each offers a slightly different view of the Everglades. The Pahayokee Trail, located 12.5 miles from the southern park entrance, is a good place to see alligators hidden amongst the sawgrass and cypress vegetation. A short boardwalk leads to an elevated observation tower, which has an accessible ramp. Seven miles down the road, the Mahogany Hammock Trail winds through a magnificent tropical mahogany jungle. There are a few slight inclines on this trail, and it's a much easier roll if you follow the trail in a counter-clockwise direction. West Lake Trail, located 30.5 miles from the south park entrance offers a nice stroll through the mangrove forest that surrounds the shallow West Lake. Raccoons, lizards, and snakes are the prevalent wildlife along this trail.

Out west, Yosemite National Park also offers a variety of accessible trails. A recent addition to the park is the accessible trail at Happy Isles. This trail is a prime example of how an accessible trail can be integrated into the existing landscape without impacting the environment. This gently sloping trail crosses the Merced River in two spots and is made of decomposed granite. Another nice trail is the trail to Mirror Lake. Although this trail gets a bit steep at the top, visitors with a disabled placard are allowed to drive on the trail. The trails around the lake vary in accessibility, but most wheelers can access some of them. It's a very peaceful place with beautiful views. Speaking of great views; one of the newest access upgrades is located at Glacier Point; about 45 minutes from the valley floor. Glacier Point is the place to get a spectacular view of the entire park; and many recent improvements, including new ramps and trails have (finally) made this Yosemite landmark nicely accessible.

And Although the natural entrance to Carlsbad Caverns is not accessible, visitors can reach the Big Room by elevator. A large section of the Big Room, (where you'll fine some spectacular rock formations) is accessible. There are a few areas that are roped off to wheelchair-users (for safety reasons) but it's still possible to see most areas of the Big Room. Additionally, there are accessible nature trails and picnic sites located near the visitor center and at nearby Rattlesnake Springs.

No matter which national park you choose to visit, advance research is a must. The best place to start is the national parks website at *www.nps.gov*. Some parks have access information listed, while others only have contact phone numbers. Sometimes you have to pick up the phone and talk directly to a park employee to find out about access.

Park rangers can be a good source of access information. For example, I've been going to Yosemite for over 40 years, but just last year I found out about Washburn Point from a ranger. Located about a half mile below Glacier Point, it's nicely accessible, has a spectacular view and is less crowded that nearby Glacier Point. The ranger knew about access because his sister is a wheelchair-user. It never hurts to ask.

Finally, if a visit to a National Park is in your future, be sure and get your free Golden Access Passport. This lifetime pass is good for free admission to all national parks, monuments, historic sites, recreation areas and wildlife refuges. Pass holders also receive a 50% discount on campsites. The Golden Access Passport can be obtained at any national park entrance or Bureau of Land Management (BLM) office. There is no charge for the Golden Access Passport, but "proof of disability" (such as a doctor's letter or SSDI check stub) is required. For more information about the golden access passport, visit *www.nps.gov* or call your local BLM office.

Campsites and Cabins—Many people like to stay in or near recreation areas. Accessible lodging choices range from camping and rustic cabins, to luxury lodges and resorts.

Although camping is the traditional way to enjoy the great outdoors, campgrounds are not always accessible. Additionally, if a campground is listed as accessible, it's a good idea to inquire about the specific access features. Most often, "accessible", means the campground has a level campsite, accessible parking and an accessible bathroom. Raised camping platforms are not the standard, so be prepared to sleep on the ground. Some campgrounds will reserve accessible campsites in advance, and some won't; again it pays to check in advance. There are also a number of accessible facilities like Bonfils Stanton and WOW that have gone the full nine yards to make their campsites accessible.

If pitching a tent isn't really your style, then consider a USDA Forest Service Cabin. They're a bit rustic, and indeed some are very basic; but, they're a great choice if you love the outdoors. They are located across the US and some are accessible, depending on when they were built or remodeled. For example, up in Alaska there are barrier-free Forest Service cabins at West Point, Kah Sheets Lake, Heckman Lake, Green Island, and Virginia Lake. Each cabin includes a table and benches, plywood bunks, a wood or oil heating stove, a broom, and an outhouse. The cabins don't have electricity, bedding, or cooking utensils. Reservations for Forest Service cabins can be made up to 180 days in advance, through the National Recreation Reservation Service.

State parks are also good resources for accessible cabins. For example, Smallwood State Park is doing a great job of providing accessible lodgings. This Maryland state park has four accessible cabins; two cabins are located in the woods and two cabins overlook the Potomac River. The cabins all have electricity and air conditioning. Visitors can also enjoy the accessible facilities of the park, including the floating marina, fixed docks, boat launch, fish cleaning stations and the pedestrian walkway along the shore.

And then there are Yurts; Oregon's version of luxury camping. Yurts are permanent domed structures with plywood floors, framed doors, electricity and skylights. They are furnished (you supply the bedding) and can sleep up to five people. They are located in many of Oregon's state campgrounds and are a bargain at $27/night (peak). Cooking is not allowed inside the yurts, but there are picnic and barbecue areas outside. Bathroom facilities are available in accessible community bathrooms. Some yurts are accessible, but you need to specify that you need an accessible yurt when you make your reservation. Reservations are a must, as yurts are popular and sell out quickly.

And if you really want to get up and close and personal with nature, consider Mala Mala safari camp in South Africa. The Mala Mala main camp is set in beautiful surroundings on the banks of the Sand River. The thatched roof buildings are located on manicured lawns and surrounded by mature shade trees. Mala Mala main camp has an accessible suite complete with ramps, wide doorways, wheelchair height furniture, and a bathroom with a roll-in shower and shower seat. The facilities were designed with the assistance of the Quadriplegic Association of South Africa, in order to meet international standards for accessibility.

Hit The Beach—A lot of recreational activities revolve around the water. Indeed, the beach is a popular recreational venue. You can choose to simply sit and enjoy the sand and surf, or opt for a refreshing dip in the ocean. Beach access varies, and includes everything from beach chairs and hard packed sand to barrier-free access by ramps. And of course there are still many beaches that are not accessible at all.

One way to access the beach is in a beach wheelchair. These specially made wheelchairs have wide plastic tires which are designed to navigate sandy beaches. The major drawback is that they are not self-propelling, so you need somebody to push you. For those people who want independent access, a beach wheelchair is not a good option. There are a variety of companies that manufacture beach wheelchairs, and you can buy your own and take it with you to the beach. They are made to disassemble easily, so they fit nicely into a car trunk or in the cargo bin of an airplane.

Many state parks, beaches and resorts also provide beach wheelchairs for loan. Although there isn't a master list of venues that provide them; some beach wheelchair dealers do have this information; so ask if they have a list of recreation areas that use their equipment. Some dealers also provide this information on-line. Do an internet search under "beach wheelchairs" and see what you find.

Beach wheelchairs are OK, but direct access to the beach is even better. Unfortunately, not many beaches have ramp access, but the ones that do are very well done. Take Luquillo Beach in Puerto Rico for example. The sand is hard-packed and negotiable in a scooter, and there is also a ramp to the water. There is an accessible walkway along the shore with access to outside showers, picnic areas and a playground. Accessible parking places, changing rooms, showers and restrooms are located at the far end of the parking lot. Luquillo Beach is one the most beautiful beaches in the Caribbean. It's also the most accessible.

Another unique approach to beach access is can be found at the Yaquina Head Tidepools, on the central Oregon coast. This coastal headland area was established by Congress in 1980; and in 1992-1994 the Bureau of Land Management (BLM) reclaimed the Yaquina Head rock quarry and converted it to a rocky intertidal area. The BLM also made the intertidal area wheelchair accessible; a first for the Oregon coast. Accessible pathways allow wheelchair users to roll along and explore the tidepools. Wheelchair-users can park in the lower parking lot, and just roll on down to the tidepools. The paved paths go right into the intertidal area. There are also a few "raised tidepools" which are just the right "viewing height" for wheelers. Yaquina Head gets high marks for barrier-free design.

Water Sports—Let's turn our attention to water sports now. From fishing to water skiing, the water attracts professional athletes and weekend amateurs alike.

Fishing continues to be a popular recreational activity. For those who prefer to fish from shore, there are many choices. In fact, access doesn't have to be elaborate. Over in Frasier, Colorado the local Lions Club constructed a very simple accessible fishing area around their local fishing hole. They did two things; first they built an accessible dock, so that wheelchair users could just roll on and fish. And second, they constructed some safety barriers that allow wheelchair-users to fish safely from shore. The wheelchair height barriers have one rail across the top; and although they prevent wheelers from rolling into the water, they don't obstruct the view. Of course they are made of natural material so they blend in with the environment.

Over in the Catskill Mountains of New York state, Project Access continues to develop barrier-free fishing areas using only shovels, rakes and wheelbarrows. Project Access provides barrier-free access and protects streams from degradation, and they encourage others to create additional barrier-free sites on rivers across the US. Project Access is also an excellent resource for locating barrier-free fishing areas. In addition to their own fishing areas in the Catskills, they also list barrier-free fishing areas across the US on their very informative website.

Water Skiing is another popular activity. Most skiers use a sit-ski, which allows skiers to ski from a seated position. Water skiing is well suited for a wide range of disabilities. Skiers first learn to master the basic moves and work on their balance. Later they progress to advanced skills such as wake-to-wake crossing, the slalom course and trick skiing. A wide variety of adaptive equipment is available for water skiing.

Disabled Sports USA (DSUSA) is the leader in adaptive water skiing instruction. Each summer they also team up with Kawasaki to present Operation Challenge; a series of National Watersports Clinics. Operation Challenge travels across the US to teach adaptive jet-skiing and water skiing, and to promote the fact that people with disabilities can participate in these sports. Kawasaki provides the jet-ski equipment, and DSUSA provides the teaching expertise. Together they make an effective teaching team. For more information on Operation challenge or DSUSA water skiing programs in your area, contact the DSUSA national headquarters.

Sailing is another fun way to enjoy the water. Passengers can sit back and enjoy a leisurely sail or they can actively participate in the navigation of the vessel. NSCD is a leader in adaptive sailing, and in 1999 they added yet another dimension to their already popular sailing program, with the addition of *Sea Legs* to their fleet. *Sea Legs* is a customized sailboat, specially constructed so it can be fully operated from a seated position. Fitted with an accessible fiberglass mold, all sailing operations can be completed from two swivel seats which allow access to the entire boat. So you don't have to be able to walk, in order to learn to sail. Sailing lessons are available at the NSCD, and no previous sailing experience is required. Graduates of the course (or any sailing course) are also eligible to rent *Sea Legs* for their own sailing experience on Lake Granby.

And if you've ever dreamed of sailing a tall ship, then check out the Jubilee Sailing Trust (JST), a UK based non-profit organization. The JST operates two accessible tall ships, the *Lord Nelson* and the *Tenacious;* and JST participants are not just passengers, they are members of the crew. Wheelers and able-bodied crew members work side by side. Accessible features on board JST ships include flat wide decks suitable for wheelchair-users, lifts between the decks, wheelchair tie downs and accessible living quarters. JST stresses integration and inclusion in all of their programs.

Another British organization, the Disabled Sailors Associations (DSA) is working hard to provide accessible sailing opportunities to more people. Their goal is to make sailing accessible for everyone. DSA designed and built the *Verity K*, the world's first wheelchair accessible 35 foot cruising yacht. The *Verity K* is available for hire by any disabled sailor, at very reasonable rates. A skipper can also be provided by the DSA for those who lack the proper sailing experience.

For those people who want to explore the undersea world, scuba diving is a great choice. The Handicapped Scuba Association (HSA) sets standards and trains instructors in adaptive techniques. They also arrange dive trips for members. Moray Wheels is a non-profit scuba club which focuses on teaching people with disabilities to dive. Both organizations are very knowledgeable about accessible dive resorts around the world.

Although many divers choose land-based vacations, another option is to live on a dive boat. Live Dive Pacific operates two accessible live aboard diving boats, the *Fiji Aggressor* and the *Kona II*. The *Fiji Aggressor* is the most accessible boat, and has, a specially-designed hydraulic skiff lift, a wheelchair elevator and shower stalls with seats. Both boats were evaluated by members of the HSA; and the Live Dive Pacific website includes access details and comments about the accessibility of both boats.

And, although it's not exactly a sport, if you want to get up close and personal with a dolphin (or two); then check out the Dolphin Research Center in Grassy Keys, Florida. This marine research center offers a "swim with the dolphins program", where participants enter a lagoon and interact with the resident dolphins. This recreational swim program is designed for people with disabilities, and open to participants of all ages. It's a very popular program, and it fills up fast, so advance reservations are a must.

Fun In The Snow—Skiing is a popular winter activity, and a ski vacation makes a great winter getaway. The good news is that there is a wide variety of adaptive equipment that helps people with all types of disabilities enjoy the excitement of downhill skiing and Nordic sports. Truly there is something for just about everybody.

Downhill skiers can either stand up or sit down to ski, depending on their ability. Stand-up skiers use outriggers for balance. Outriggers are modified ski poles with "little skis" attached to the ends. Three track skiers use one ski and two outriggers, while four track skiers use two skis and two outriggers. Sometimes a ski bra is also used in conjunction with this technique, to help skiers control the position of their ski tips.

Sit-down skiers can use either a mono-ski, a bi-ski or a sit-ski. A mono-ski is a fiberglass shell and a monoshock, mounted on top of a single ski. Mono skiers use two shortened outriggers to steer and turn the mono-ski. Mono-skis are a good choice for people who have disabilities affecting their legs, but still have some upper body strength. A bi-ski is constructed much like a mono-ski, except the bi-ski is mounted on two skis. This extra ski offers added stability and balance. Bi-skis are used by people who have limited upper body strength, along with limited or no lower body strength. A bi-skier may ski independently or may be tethered (pulled) by an instructor. A sit-ski is a sled-like piece of adaptive equipment, which is used by people who have very limited or no mobility. The sit-ski is tethered at all times, but sometimes skiers are able to assist in steering the sit-ski, by using a ski pole.

Although downhill skiing is a long-standing winter favorite, the Nordic sports are also very popular. So if downhill skiing isn't your cup of tea, then consider cross country skiing or snowshoeing. Both are great fun and offer a good aerobic workout.

And although not really considered a Nordic sport, snowboarding is fast becoming the "cool" winter sport of the younger set.

Cross country skiing is great exercise for both stand-up and sit-down skiers, and it can be adapted for a wide range of disabilities. It gets you "away from the maddening crowds" and, depending on your luck and location, can allow you an up-close and personal glimpse of the local wildlife. Remember to pack your binoculars, as you never know what you will see. Many hand cyclists and wheelchair racers take up cross country skiing to stay in shape during the winter; however you don't have to be a super athlete to enjoy this sport.

Participants who can stand up, use traditional cross country skiing equipment; long narrow skis with bindings which attach to the toe of the boot. Skiers who can't stand-up, walk, or have problems maintaining their balance use a sit-ski. Sit-skiers propel themselves with shortened ski poles in this adapted sled-like device. Equipment makers are now developing new sit-skis that add "kick" to each push, resulting in more slide for each arm movement. Of course, most adaptive ski schools are pros at altering and tweaking existing equipment to meet individual needs, so don't be afraid to call them up, and ask what they can do for you.

Snowshoeing is another sport that can get you away from the crowds, and into some lovely forested areas. It's quite an aerobic workout, more so than walking, as snowshoes tend to sink into the powdery snow. Snowshoers need to be able to walk with independent leg action, although poles or outriggers can be used to help a bit with balance. Snowshoeing is also a great sport for people who are blind or who have low vision.

And although adaptive technology hasn't quite caught up with snowboarding (yet), it's still great fun. Participants need to be able to stand-up, use their legs and balance themselves; however there are some minor adaptations that can be made to the equipment, such as moving the bindings. Some people also use outriggers to help maintain their balance. The good news is that several individuals and organizations are working to develop adaptive equipment for non-ambulatory snowboarders. For now, snowboarding is best suited for people who have sensory or cognitive disabilities, but as technology improves look for more adaptive equipment for people with mobility disabilities.

Adaptive snow sports are available in the US, Canada, Europe, New Zealand and Australia. Two good adaptive skiing resources are DSUSA and the NSCD. Additionally the Emerging Horizons website (EmergingHorizons.com) has an updated list of adaptive ski schools around the world. Most adaptive ski schools will custom tailor equipment to meet individual needs. For best results, check with the facility in advance, explain your disability in detail, and find out what equipment is available.

Before You Go—It goes without saying that advance research is necessary before you hit the road, however; there's another important aspect to consider whenever recreation is a major part of your holiday. Always remember to take any recreational equipment or adaptive devices with you. Indeed, sometimes this takes just as much planning as your travel arrangements. This point is aptly illustrated by the following story from Patty, an above the knee amputee who wanted to enjoy the water on her family vacation.

"We planned to spend a week at a lakefront resort in upstate New York. My son's baseball team was playing a tournament in Cooperstown, so this wasn't only a family vacation, but also a vacation for the families of all my son's teammates. As we made our plans, I realized that most of our non-baseball time would revolve around fun in the pool and lake. We have two young boys and I didn't want to be a spectator to their activities; but as a bilateral above the knee amputee, I wasn't sure how much I could participate."

"Sure I swim at home. In fact, I have a set of water legs that are specifically designed for water activities. My water legs allow me to swim, water ski, jet ski, sail and generally enjoy the water. I've used my water legs at home, but I had never traveled with them before. My problem was pretty simple; I just couldn't figure out how to transport my water legs from California to New York."

"I couldn't imagine my husband carrying them down the aisle of the airplane. I wasn't even sure if they'd fit in the overhead bin. If not, I wondered if they would survive the trip in the cargo bin. I've had nightmare airline experiences with my wheelchair and I didn't want to repeat those with my water legs. Would insurance cover damage to my water legs? Who would take responsibility if they were damaged? I had a lot of questions, and very few answers. So, I called my prosthetist."

"'How do I get my water legs to New York?' I asked. 'Simple,' he responded, 'we'll ship them.' As instructed, I delivered my water legs to my prosthetist, one week before we left. Upon arrival, they were waiting for me when I checked into the hotel. There was also a return-shipping label, a roll of packing tape and even a pair of scissors inside the box. It was obvious they had done this before! I enjoyed my water legs during my vacation. I spent a considerable amount of time in the pool, and I was glad I brought them."

So, even if it takes a little extra work before and after your trip, make sure you take along everything you need to make your vacation enjoyable. You'll be glad you did. And, don't be afraid to ask others for advice. They may have just the solution you need!

14 | Budget Travel

Is It Really Possible?

Is it really possible to travel on a budget? Well of course, that depends on your budget. Seriously though, it never hurts to stretch you travel dollar; and to some people "budget travel" simply means "getting the best deal possible." To others, budget travel has a more concrete definition; usually a dollar amount per day or per trip. So, is it really possible to travel on a limited budget without sacrificing access? The answer is a qualified "yes". It is possible to put a cap on travel expenses, and still get the accessible services you need; however, don't expect to get five star service for a two star price. Like everything else, budget travel requires planning and research, and sometimes a little compromise. But the good news is, it is possible. Access and affordability don't have to be mutually exclusive.

What is Budget Travel?—In order to better understand travel costs, let's take a look at two different trips to the same destination. The first trip is a hotel and air package deal and the second trip is an all inclusive guided tour. Both tours are accessible, and use the same hotel. The guided tour includes private tours each day in an accessible minivan and the hotel package includes a half day sightseeing tour on an accessible bus. The hotel package costs $800 per person and the guided tour costs $1500 per person. Why?

Well, in this case you are paying for service; more specifically the service of your own personal tour guide in a private vehicle. Is it worth the extra cost? It depends on what you want. If you truly want an all inclusive escorted tour, then it's usually easier to join a guided tour then to arrange things on your own. On the other hand if you just want to explore the city yourself, you're probably paying for unneeded services if you join a guided tour. At first glance the hotel package seems like a deal, but if you plan to tour the city extensively, the hotel package becomes less of a bargain. The first rule of budget travel is to pay only for the services you need; but, don't forget to figure in all the associated costs before you pick the best deal.

Choosing Your Destination—People choose vacation destinations for a variety of reasons, including wheelchair-access. Although it pays to choose an accessible destination, sometimes that just isn't possible. Not every country is as accessible as the US; and even within the US borders some cities are just more accessible than others. On the other hand, you should be aware that the level of access at your destination can raise or lower your vacation expenses.

For example, lets say you choose to go to a relatively inaccessible third world country. Let's assume there is no accessible public transportation available in this country, but there is one tour company that has an adapted van. In short that's the only way you will be able to tour that country; in the adapted van. You will also need the services of a tour escort, because many of the attractions and hotels have steps, and you'll need to be lifted up and down them in your wheelchair. Is this a budget trip? No, and quite frankly the only thing you can do to change that is to find a more accessible destination.

Remember this rule. The relative accessibility of any destination, along with the availability of local accessible transportation and tour services is a major factor in determining the cost of any trip. In the above case, the cost will be higher because of the high level of personal assistance required and because of the lack of competition among accessible tour operators. This is usually true in any country that does not have a high level of accessible facilities and services.

Choosing a more accessible destination usually helps rein in travel costs. This doesn't mean that you have to stick with US destinations; but some compromises may be needed in order to lower your vacation costs. Truly, if your dream vacation is to go to the furthest reaches of Nepal, then go for it; however, realize that this is not the budget option. Decide if you can compromise on a destination. If so, then look for ways to make it on your budget. If you can't compromise on a destination, then go for it, but realize you will pay more. The more flexibility you have destination wise, the more money you'll save. It's often a good idea to pick several destinations, and then go with the one that offers the best travel deal.

Timing is Everything—It goes without saying that travel costs rise during peak travel times; so for the best deals it pays to travel in the off season. So when is the off season? Well, that depends on a number of things, including your destination.

Travel prices rise drastically during the holidays; in fact it's the most expensive time to travel, even if you stay with family. However, it's hard to postpone the holidays, so sometimes travel during this time is essential. What do you do then? If you must travel around the holidays, then start shopping early for your air ticket. Watch the airfare sales and snap up you ticket early in the year. Don't wait until the month before Thanksgiving to buy your air ticket.

If you don't have to travel during Christmas and Thanksgiving, and your schedule is flexible; then a little research can help lower your travel costs. The first step is to determine the peak travel season for you destination. This varies from destination to destination. A good way to determine the peak season is to look at lodging and resort rates for your destination. Most have high, low and shoulder season rates listed, along with a definition of each season. Check several resorts in the same area in order

CANDY HARRINGTON

to get a good idea of when the peak and low seasons occur. The best time to travel is not usually in the low season, but in the shoulder season. That's because the low season is usually the low season for a very good reason. Many times it's weather related. Additionally, in some resort areas many of the attractions are closed during the low season.

Then there's what MSNBC's Peter Greenberg calls the "dead week", the 10 days following New Years Day. During this time, virtually every segment of the travel business offers substantial discounts. It's a great time to take a vacation. You'll find good deals on hotel rooms, air fares and cruise packages. It's also a nice time to travel because not many people travel during this time. In fact that's why there are so many deep discounts. It's a simple case of supply and demand. During this time, most people are just returning to work from their holiday excursions. The Christmas bills are coming in, and most people just don't think about travel at this time. So, if you want to grab a really good deal, plan ahead, be flexible and travel during the dead week.

Airfares—In truth there is no magic formula for finding the lowest airfare. Of course that statement is nothing short of blasphemy to many people. Everybody has their own "tried and true" method. I have friends who subscribe to virtually every airline e-mail list, and those that use complicated software programs. I even know people that call up 12 different travel agents every week until they find a bargain. And they all have their own rules, like, "Never book a ticket on the third Monday of any month that begins with the letter 'J'." Of course they all swear that their own method is the only "real" way to good deal. I don't buy it. I mean, why don't I just swing a garlic necklace over my head three times, face north and hit the "book your fare now" button. To me, it all seems like a lot of trouble. Life is just too short.

I use the common sense approach. In my book, there are two simple rules for finding the lowest airfare. First you have to know the regular price of the airfare to your destination. Second, you have to accept the fact that somebody on the airplane probably got a better deal than you did. Otherwise, shopping for a bargain airfare becomes an obsession. My method is pretty simple. Just decide when and where you want to travel. You also need to know the regular price of the airfare, so you'll be able to recognize a good deal. Check the prices on the internet weekly until you find your best fare. Then buy the ticket, and don't look back.

Where is the best place to check airfares on-line? Well, I prefer the airline websites, because I know what I'm getting. I know I'm not comparing apples to oranges when I'm looking at two different airfares. I'm able to see the aircraft type, routings and seating diagrams on the airline websites; and these are all critical factors when I choose a flight. In most cases, you do get what you pay for, in regards to airfares. In my opinion an airfare is no longer a bargain if I have to fly in a turbo prop and change planes three times. You'll also find sales and special deals on airline websites; deals that you won't find in other places. It really doesn't matter which airline website you use. Choose your favorite airline or check several competitors; but, remember to use a US flag air carrier in order to insure access mandated under the Air Carriers Access Act (ACAA).

Of course, it pays to fly in the shoulder or low seasons. Additionally try to fly midweek. Tuesdays and Wednesdays are usually the best days for the lowest airfares. Business travelers pay the highest airfares, so flights on Monday and Friday are usually the most expensive. Finally, shop around for airfare and hotel packages; as sometimes these deals offer hefty discounts on both the airfare and the hotel rates. If you choose this option, you'll need to find out what hotels are used by the airline and then investigate their access on your own. A word of warning here; never rely on the airlines for hotel access information!

Attendant Airfare Discounts—Wouldn't it be great to get free airfare for your attendant? Now, that would really reduce your travel costs, wouldn't it? Well, it's a nice dream, but in reality that's all it is; a dream. The cold hard truth is that no airlines offer this perk. Furthermore, US air carriers are not required to do so under the ACAA. In truth, there's a lot of misunderstanding about the law, so here's a synopsis of what the ACAA has to say about the subject.

Under the ACAA, US air carriers may require some passengers to travel with an attendant. This includes passengers who have a disability so severe that they can't assist with their own emergency evacuation. It also includes passengers who are unable to receive and act on necessary instructions in the event of an emergency. That's a pretty broad definition, and in the end it's a judgment call on the part of the crew. In short, a US air carrier can require a passenger to travel with an attendant, even if the passenger assures airline personnel that he can travel independently. However, the air carrier cannot charge for the transportation of an airline-required attendant.

That doesn't exactly mean that you can select your own attendant though. The air carrier can opt to designate an off duty employee as your attendant. Airline personnel can even ask for a volunteer on the flight to be your attendant. Sounds good, right? Well, here's the big catch. The airline-required attendant is not required to provide any type of personal service to the passenger. The sole duty of an airline-required attendant is to provide assistance to the passenger in the event of an emergency evacuation. In short, an airline-required attendant won't help you eat but he will get you off the plane if it crashes. The bottom line is that US airlines can require an attendant to travel with you, they can assign the attendant, and they can limit the duties of the attendant. Additionally the airlines are not required to find an attendant for you if they deem you must travel with one for safety reasons. In this case, they can simply deny you passage. You can see why this law is so often misinterpreted.

Although there's no such thing as free air travel for attendants, a few airlines do offer discounted travel. As with everything airline-related, some restrictions do apply, so contact the air carriers directly for more information. Currently no US airlines offer discounted attendant travel, but here's the latest rundown of non US air carriers that do offer some sort of attendant fares.

Air Canada offers some reduced fares for attendant travel. The attendant must be able to care for the passenger during the flight, and the reduced fare is limited in availability. British Midland offers a 50% discount to companions of blind travelers. The fare is further limited to passengers traveling for business, charitable or health reasons. Quantas Airlines offers the Qantas Carer Concession Card scheme, which enables people with high support needs and their attendants to travel at reduced rates. Through this scheme, both the person with high support needs and their attendant are able to travel at 50% off any full priced domestic Qantas flight. The Qantas Carer Concession Card scheme is administered by NICAN. Certain conditions and restrictions apply. Contact the airlines directly for more information on these attendant discounts.

Lodging—Another way to stretch your travel dollar is to rein in those ever-escalating lodging costs. According to PKF consulting, a San Francisco based travel research firm, hotel rates have increased 37% since 1995. The good news is, it's still possible to find lodging that's both affordable and accessible. I've already covered some budget lodging options such as hostels and home exchanges in the "Finding The Right Room" chapter; however there are few other ways to lower your lodging costs.

First off, consider the location of your hotel. Generally speaking you will pay more for hotels in the city center than those out in the suburbs. However, make sure that it won't cost you more in transportation costs to get to the city center, if you do choose a suburban hotel. Sometimes it's just more economical to pay the higher city hotel rates if there are no accessible public transportation options nearby. Additionally, don't forget to ask about senior discounts, auto club rates or other special deals when booking a room. Sometimes special discounts aren't widely advertised and it never hurts to ask.

As far as hotels go, many hotel chains, such as Microtel and Motel 6, offer accessible rooms at reasonable rates. Microtel gets the highest marks for consistent access, as all Microtel properties are constructed from the ground up with access in mind. Their goal is to be the preferred motel chain for travelers with disabilities. So far they've done a great job. Their rates start at $32. Visit the Microtel website for a virtual tour of an accessible room.

Motel 6 can also offer good access, but unfortunately they're not very consistent. When they're good, they're very, very good; but when they're bad, you have to almost be a contortionist to use the toilet. Most of their newly constructed (post ADA) properties are nicely accessible, so look for properties constructed after 1992. Their remodeled properties are access nightmares, so make sure and ask a lot of questions before you book a room. Their rates start at a very affordable $45.99.

And if your travels take you across the Big Pond, you can't beat Travel Inns for access and value in the United Kingdom. Says Ann Litt of Undiscovered Britain, "All Travel Inns have at least a couple of adapted rooms which have wide doorways, grab bars, adapted bathrooms and low rise tubs. They're not luxury properties, but they are clean, affordable and accessible." Rates start at $58.

Of course, you can always look to the great outdoors for some budget lodging options. If that's your choice, don't leave home without your Golden Access Passport, a free lifetime pass available to any US resident with a permanent disability. Pass holders get free admission to all national parks, and a 50% discount on campsites. For more information about the Golden Access Passport, contact your local Bureau of Land Management office or visit the National Parks Service website. Golden Access Passports are available at all national park entrances.

Transportation—One of the most expensive components of any trip is accessible ground transportation. Many people don't even consider this as a cost of travel because sometimes it's added into the cost of a group tour. But even if you don't see it as an itemized cost, the high cost of accessible ground transportation helps push up the price of many tours.

Why is accessible transportation so expensive? According to one veteran accessible tour operator, skyrocketing insurance costs are to blame for the high cost of accessible transportation. In fact this tour operator bought a bus, converted it and made it accessible. She then had to let it sit because the insurance was so expensive. She eventually sold her bus to a bus company that gutted it and converted it back to it's original non-accessible incarnation.

One option for many accessible small tour operators is to lease an accessible bus. The down side is that accessible buses are in short supply, and the leasing companies also have to pay high insurance costs. The result? These high costs are passed on to the tour operator and ultimately to their customers. Although US tour operators are not allowed to charge a person with a disability more than an able-bodied person for the same tour; sometimes accessible specialty tours are more expensive to all customers. The reason is that once you make a tour vehicle accessible, you do loose a number of seats; and in order for tour operators to make a profit, sometimes they have to raise the price per seat.

It's hard to fault the tour operators for this, as they are really caught in the middle. Additionally some accessible tour operators provide an excellent service, and in the end that's really what you are paying for; the service. So, shop around for accessible tours, but realize that if the tour involves transportation in an accessible bus, it will most likely raise the price. In truth tour operators are caught between a rock and a hard spot here. Ultimately it's the insurance companies that are raking in the dough!

So, what's a traveler to do? Well if you're on a budget, you might want to consider booking a few day tours in an accessible vehicle, instead of opting for a fully escorted tour. Check around for accessible public transportation options in your destination city. Taxis can sometimes be hired for half day sightseeing tours, and many taxis are accessible. Additionally you might want to rent your own self drive accessible van for a few days. Again, this is not a cheap option, as most accessible vans run $100 (or more) per day; however, you may only need to rent one for a few days if you organize your activities appropriately. Research makes the difference, so investigate your accessible transportation options long before you depart for the airport. Your pre-trip research could translate into valuable savings.

Cruises—Cruises are a popular travel option, and like everything else it pays to be flexible with your travel dates and destinations for the best cruise deals. Additionally there are a few things your should understand about cruise pricing, in order to maximize your savings.

First off, the brochure price of a cruise is pretty comparable to the sticker price of a car. In short it's like the "suggested retail price", and most cruise passengers pay less than the brochure price. In fact, some passengers pay substantially less than the brochure price. How do they do that? Well, the best way to get a good price on your dream cruise is to work with a travel agent that monitors cruise prices (at least) weekly.

Cruise prices rise and fall like the stock market, even though the general public isn't always aware of these fluctuations. It's a simple case of supply and demand, and most price fluctuations are based on cabin availability. Once you book a cruise you're locked into that price; however, if your travel agent finds a lower rate before you sail, she can re-book you, lock you into the lower price and save you big bucks. Of course this plan of action only works if your travel agent monitors cruise prices frequently. Additionally it works best when you book your cruise at least six months to a year in advance. It's also important to note that even though your cruise price can't increase once you're locked into a specific rate; other fees such as government taxes, port charges and airline fuel surcharges can still increase.

Another way to save some bucks on a cruise is to look for repositioning cruises. These are fairly well publicized by the cruise lines and they usually occur at the end of the season, when the cruise lines move (reposition) their ships to different routes. The cruise lines have to get their ships from port A to port B to start their new cruise schedule, and it's a great marketing move to also sell the cabins at bargain prices. The downside of a repositioning cruise is that open-jaw airfares (when you fly into one city and out of another one) are sometimes rather expensive. In fact these higher airfares can sometimes offset any cruise savings.

It also pays to let your travel agent know as much about you as possible. Let her know where you live, how old you are and if you have ever cruised before. These seemingly mundane details can actually be the ticket to big savings in the form of special regional fares, senior specials or alumni fares. And finally, don't forget to tell your travel agent if you plan to travel with some friends; as sometimes you can earn a free cabin just by putting together a group cruise.

Be Your Own Tour Guide—Another way to save a few bucks on your travel costs is to be your own tour guide; however this is only a realistic option for those people who have the time and inclination to thoroughly research their destinations. To some people it's just more trouble than it's worth; and quite frankly some people would rather pay for the services of a tour guide than to spend their valuable time researching access. To others it's the ticket to savings.

Of course the first step to being your own tour guide starts well before you ever leave home. In fact, valuable time can be lost just getting your bearings in a strange city. To that end, pre-trip research is essential. I'm constantly reminded of the saga of my friend John, who spent five days in Paris last Spring. Indeed, most of the tour companies told him that this would be an adequate amount of time for him to see his favorite attractions; however, John opted to be his own tour guide and he wasted the first two days looking for a good city map. He did no pre-trip research. The result? He spent most of his time getting his bearings, trying to figure out the metro and showing up at attractions that were closed. It was a very disappointing trip for John. The moral of the story is to have your itinerary pretty well mapped out before you hit the road. Study a city map in advance and have a good idea about public transportation options, and the operating hours of the major attractions. And don't forget to pack the map!

So, where do you start with your pre trip research? A good first stop is the local convention and visitors bureau. In addition to detailed city maps and information on local attractions; some convention and visitors bureaus also publish access guides, so don't forget to ask about access information. You might also want to check with the local chamber of commerce. Contact these resources well in advance and have them mail the tourist information to you. Additionally you may also want to stop in at the visitors center once you arrive, just to make sure there's nothing you missed. How do you find a local convention and visitors bureau? One good resource is the on-line directory at *www.ChamberofCommerce.com.*

Of course it also pays to surf the internet and ask friends and family for resources too. Don't forget to look for free factory tours. A wide variety of businesses offer these free tours; from jelly bean factories to breweries, and many are accessible. Many major museums also have free days every week or month. Find out when these are, in order to cut down on sightseeing costs. And remember, the free Golden Access Passport is also good for free admittance to national monuments too. Of course it never hurts to ask about unpublished specials or discounts. Some special rates only apply to certain days or hours. Indeed, this is where that pre trip research adds up to some big savings.

Deal Direct And Save—Of course, no matter what the product, the best way to get the lowest price is to deal direct and save. As far as travel is concerned, sometimes that's easier said than done. The ultimate goal is to hire your own local tour operator in order to maximize your savings. Tour operators usually pay a commission to travel agents; and many times if a commission is involved, it's just cheaper to deal direct.

The first step is to hunt down the local tour operators. One way is to browse through US tour company brochures. Sometimes they mention the name of the local tour operator or sometimes there is a photograph of a tour vehicle with the local company logo. It doesn't hurt to ask the US agent who the local tour operator is; but don't expect any type of useful reply. In fact you may meet with some resistance from the US agent; however it never hurts to ask. Sometimes agents are willing to give out this information, even if it's only to get you off the phone.

And finally, ask friends, family and business contacts if they have any resources. Don't forget to investigate every possibility; as you never know when something will pan out. I've made many good contacts with what I at first thought were questionable referrals. The goal is to find somebody at your destination that has access to information on local tour operators. Sometimes this involves quite a number of contacts. But don't give up, as the internet has truly opened up the world, as it allows for a free exchange of valuable information. The best advice is to be persistent and remember to be methodical in your quest.

15 | Resources

Years ago, travel opportunities for people with disabilities were pretty limited. Today, things have changed, and more and more wheelers are hitting the road. Due to this change, the demand for accurate access information has reached an all time high; and (fortunately) new access resources are popping up every day. So where do you begin your search for these resources?

Well, of course my favorite resource is *Emerging Horizons*. In fact, that's why I founded the magazine; to provide updated information on barrier-free travel. Along with legal updates and access news, I give *Emerging Horizons* readers travel tips, new resources and specific access information about destinations. And believe me, we do go out and research all of our destination pieces. Rest assured that we don't rely on second-hand access information or press releases. We actually investigate the access first-hand. If there's one thing I've learned about access information over the years, it's that you can't rely on third or fourth-hand information. Something always gets lost in the translation. So, the next time you read an article about access, find out if the writer actually visited the destination before you accept the information as fact. It will save you a lot of grief. All right, that's the end of my *Emerging Horizons* commercial!

Through the course of my research for *Emerging Horizons*, I've also stumbled across a number of other potential sources of access information. Take note that I said "potential" sources. In fact, sometimes you'll completely strike out with these sources, however it never hurts to ask.

One of my favorite sources for updated access information is the local Center for Independent Living (CIL). Check with the CIL in your destination city to see if they have any access information on local transportation, attractions and lodging. You might also want to contact some national disability organizations to see if they have any access information. Be sure to hit up any disability related organizations that recently held a conference (or are planning to hold a conference) in your destination city. Many such organizations collect local access information for their conference attendees. Don't forget about airports and public transportation providers, as sometimes they also provide print access guides. And finally, don't rule out the local Convention and Visitors Bureaus (CVB). Some CVBs incorporate access information in their own tourism publications, while other CVBs work with local organizations to provide this information in separate access guides.

Print Access Guides and Resources—Access guides come in a variety of forms. For example, in 2000 Access Northern California published San Francisco's first access guide. Today, the San Francisco CVB continues to make this valuable resource available to all visitors. The guide contains detailed access information on hotels, restaurants, museums, public transportation, theaters, tourist attractions and shopping centers. It's available free from the San Francisco Convention and Visitors Bureau at (415) 391-2000. You can also order a copy on-line at *www.AccessNCA.com*. Access Northern California continues to publish updated editions of the guide.

Many CVBs publish local access guides. Get your copy of *Access San Francisco* to find out about access to Alcatraz Island (pictured here), as well as other local attractions.

And down in Palm Springs, Palm Springs Tourism worked with the Palm Springs ADA Coordinator, to produce *A Mobility Impaired Traveler's Guide to Palm Springs*. This guide features detailed access information on selected lodgings in Palm Springs, along with general access information on the major tourist attractions. It's available free from the Palm Springs Visitor Information center at (800) 347-7746.

The Virginia Tourism Corporation continues to publish yearly updates of *The Virginia Travel Guide for Persons with Disabilities*. This access guide contains travel resources such as dialysis centers, oxygen sources and equipment repair facilities; along with information on accessible transportation, attractions, lodgings and restaurants. It covers the entire state of Virginia. *The Virginia*

Travel Guide for Persons with Disabilities is available free from the Virginia Tourism Corporation at (800) 742-3935.

Accessible San Diego (ASD) also produces annual updates of *Access in San Diego*. This guide contains access information on selected hotels, restaurants, public transportation and tourist attractions. There is a charge for the guide, and it's only available through ASD. For more information call ASD at (858) 279-5119.

Another good general resource is Pat Smither's *Around The World Resource Guide*. Pat updates the book annually and it's filed with listings and contact information for publications, travel agents, disability websites, and access guides. The *Around The World Resource Guide* is available from Access for Disabled Americans at (925) 932-9001. Contact Access for Disabled Americans for current pricing information.

Internet Resources—Even though I think print guides are great, the best place to look for the most updated information is on the internet. Because of the nature of the medium, the internet is just more conducive to frequent updates. I didn't make up the rules, I just report them. I fully realize that there are some people out there who want nothing to do with the internet; however, if you totally exclude this medium you'll also miss out on some great access resources.

That doesn't necessarily mean you have to run out and buy a computer. In fact you can easily log on at your local library, or use a friend's computer. If you've never surfed the internet before, it's best to give it a trial run before you decide to invest in your own equipment. And by all means remember, the internet is just one source of information; and it's best used in conjunction with information from other mediums.

So where do you look on the internet. Well, although an internet search under "accessible travel" will return a bevy of selections; sometimes it's best to start out in a more directed way. Check out some of the new disability portals, as travel is a popular subject and most of them (at least) have a list of accessible travel resources. Of course websites can come and go quickly. It's just the nature of the medium; however here are a few accessible travel resources that have been around for awhile.

- Gimp on the Go—*www.GimpontheGo.com*
- Access-Able—*www.access-able.com*
- Global Access—*www.geocities.com/Paris/1502*

And then there is Emerging Horizons. Of course we have a website! In fact, we have a searchable database of accessible travel resources on our website at EmergingHorizons.com. I check the resources every month and delete outdated entries and add new ones. Feel free to drop by and browse our travel resources, and drop me an e-mail if you have a resource to suggest. Bear in mind that we don't accept any advertising on our website, and all Emerging Horizons' resources must contain specific information on accessible travel.

Chapter By Chapter Resources—Here's a chapter by chapter rundown of the resources (along with complete contact information) that are mentioned throughout the book.

On a Wing and a Prayer

Protecting Your Equipment

TravelMate Scooter
Amigo Mobility, Inc.
6693 Dixie Highway
Brideport, MI 48722
phone: (877) 292-6446
fax: (800) 334-7274
www.travelscooters.com

Gypsy Scooter
Compact Mobility Company
6140 Mid-Metro Dr., Ste. 6
Ft. Myers, FL 33912
phone: (941) 458-9290
fax: (941) 458-9298
www.compactmobility.com

Roamer Riding Chair
Wheelchair Carrier, Inc.
726 Farnsworth Road
Waterville, OH 43566
phone: (419) 878-8511
fax: (419) 878-9438
www.wheelchaircarrier.com

Scoot Around North America
396 Furby Street
Winnipeg Manitoba, Canada R3B 2V5
phone: (888) 441-7575
fax: (204) 772-6299
www.scootaround.com

Haseltine Flyer
Haseltine Corporation
phone: (888) 445-8751
www.haseltine.com

Up Up and Away

Beyond Wheelchairs

Breathin' Easy
Jerry Gorby
Breathin' Easy Publications
225 Daisy Drive
Napa, California 94558
Phone: (707) 252-9333
Fax: (707) 252-3028
www.breathineasy.com

Better Breathers Traveler
American Lung Association of San Diego and Imperial Counties
2750 Fourth Avenue
San Diego, CA 92103
Phone: (619) 297-3901

International Ventilator Users Network (IVUN)
Gazette International Networking Institute (GINI)
4207 Lindell Boulevard, #110
Saint Louis, MO 63108-2915
Phone: (314) 534-0475
Fax: (314) 534-5070
www.post-polio.org

Guide Dog Users Inc.
14311 Astrodome Dr.
Silver Springs, MD, 20906
phone: (888) 858-1008

Getting Around On the Ground

Project Action
700 13th Street N.W.,Suite 200
Washington, D.C. 2005
Phone: (202) 347-3066
fax: (202) 347-4157
www.projectaction.org

ILRU Program at TIRR
2323 S. Shepherd, Suite 1000
Houston, TX 77019
phone: (713) 520-0232
fax: (713) 520-5785

Renting Cars With Hand Controls
users.actcom.co.il/~swfm

AKA Limousine
1447 Los Meadows Street
Las Vegas, NV 89110
phone: (702) 257-7433
fax: (702) 531-5452
www.handycappedlimousine.com

RV Companion
Page Publishing Inc.
PO Box 174
Loveland CO 80539
phone: (970) 663-3295
fax: (970) 663-3550

We Will Ride

Bus Travel

Greyhound Bus
ADA Assistance Line: (800) 752-4841

All Aboard

Train Travel

Access Amtrak
phone: (877) 268-7252
www.amtrak.com

VIA Rail
phone: (888) 842-7245 (US)
phone: (800) 561-8630 (Canada)
www.viarail.ca

BritRail
phone: (877) 677-1066 (US)
phone: 08457 484950 (United Kingdom)

Eurostar
phone: 01233 617575 (United Kingdom)
www.eurostar.co.uk

Smooth Ride Guide to the UK
Smooth Ride Guides
Duck Street Barns
Furnex Pelham
Herts SG9 0LA
England

phone: 01279 777966
fax: 01279 777995

Rail Australia
phone: (8) 8217-4681
fax: (8) 8217-4682
www.railaustralia.com.au

Finding The Right Room

A Resource Guide For Hotels and Motels
CAT/UB Products
University of Buffalo
515 Kimball Tower
Buffalo, NY 14214,
phone: (800) 628-2281
fax: (716) 829-3217

Innseekers
phone: (888) Inn-Seek
www.innseekers.com

Hostelling International
733 15th Street, NW, Suite 840
Washington DC 20005
phone: (202) 783-6161
fax: (202) 783-6171
www.hiayh.org

Stockholm CIL Vacation Home Swap Bulletin Board
www.independentliving.org/vacex/index.html

So You Want To Get Off The Ship?

Cruise Travel

The Cruise Ship Center
www.cruise2.com

Wheelchair Taxi Service (Bermuda)
phone: (441) 236-1456
fax: (441) 236-7920

Anticipation Tours (Puerto Rico)
phone: (787) 630-3030 or (787) 315-7874
www.anticipationtours.com/taxi.htm

Wheelchair Getaways (Puerto Rico)
phone: (787) 883-0131
fax: (787) 883-0177

Group Tours International (Bahamas)
phone: (242) 356-4625

Dial-A-Ride (St. Thomas)
phone: (340) 776-1277
fax: (340) 777-5383

Wheelcoach Services (St. Croix)
phone: (340) 719-9335
fax: (340) 773-1414

Foster-Ince Cruise Services (Barbados)
phone: (246) 431-8921
fax: (246) 436-8908

Sam's Taxi Tours (St. Vincent)

phone: (784) 458-3686

Stockport Canal Boat Trust (UK)
Booking Agent
phone: 01663 742796

Bassingstoke Canal Boats (UK)
Judith or David Gerry
phone: 01252 622520

Lyneal Trust (UK)
The Manager
phone: 01588 638234
Saoirse ar an Uisce (Ireland)
phone: 502 43744
fax: : 502 43811

MV Dresden
Peter Deilmann EuropAmerica Cruises
1800 Diagonal Rd/ Suite 170
Alexandria, VA 22314
phone: (703) 549 1741
Fax: (703) 549 7924

Le Boat
10 South Franklin Turnpike, Suite 204 B
Ramsey, NJ 07446
Phone: (800) 992-0291
fax: :(201) 236-1214

Beyond The USA

Accessible Transportation Directorate

Canadian Transportation Agency
Ottawa, Ontario K1A 0N9
Canada
phone: (819) 997-6828
fax: (819) 953-6019

Access Canada
Alberta Hotel Association
www.albertahotels.ab.ca

RADAR
phone: 207 2503222
fax: 207 2500212
www.radar.org.uk

National Rehabilitation Board
25 Clyde Road, Ballsbridge
Dublin 4
Ireland
phone: 668 4181

Undiscovered Britain
11978 Audubon Place
Philadelphia, PA 19116
phone: (215) 969-0542
www.UndiscoveredBritain.com

Holiday Care
phone: 1293 774535
fax: 1293 784647

CBF
123 A D-64293
Darmstadt, Germany
phone: 6151 81220

fax: 6151 812281

CNRH
236 bis, rue de Tolbiac
75013 Paris
France
phone: 53 80 66 66
fax : 53 80 66 67
whanditel.jouve.fr

MOVADO
Langhansstraße 64
13086 Berlin
Germany
phone: 3047 15145
fax: 3047 31111
www.movado.de

Barrier Free Travel
Via Benedetto da Foiano, 19
50125 Florence
Italy
phone/fax: 233 5543
barrierfreetravel@tin.it

NICAN
PO Box 407
Curtin ACT 2605
Australia
phone: (2) 6285 3713
fax: (2) 6285 3714
www.nican.com.au

Easy Access Australia
Bruce Cameron

PO Box 218
Kew, Victoria 3101
Australia
fax: (3) 9853 9000

The Wheelie's Handbook of Australia
Colin James
3 Furner Avenue
Bell Park, Victoria 3215
Australia

Enable Tourism New Zealand
34 Whittaker Street
Shannon
New Zealand
phone: (6) 362 7163
fax: (6) 362 7162

Magellans
110 W. Sola Street
Santa Barbara, CA 93101
phone: (800) 962-4943
www.magellans.com

Medic Alert
phone: (888) 633-4298
www.medicalert.org

Disabled Peoples' International
www.dpi.org

Accessible Recreation

A World of Choices

National Sports Center for the Disabled
P.O. Box 1290
Winter Park, CO 80482
phone: (970) 726-1540
www.nscd.org

Wilderness on Wheels
3131 S. Vaughn Way, #305
Aurora, CO 80014
phone: (303) 751-3959

Rails to Trails Conservancy (National Headquarters)
phone: (202) 331-9696
www.railtrails.org

Trail Link Database
www.traillink.com

National Parks Service
www.nps.gov

National Recreation Reservation Service
phone: (877) 444-6777 (US)
Phone: (518) 885-3639 (outside the US)

Smallwood State Park
phone: (301) 888-1410

Oregon Yurts
phone: (800) 452-5687

Mala Mala Game Reserve
Box 2575
Randburg 2125,
South Africa
phone: (11) 789 2677
fax: (11) 886 4382
www.malamala.com

Yaquina Head Outstanding Natural Area
PO Box 936
Newport, OR 97365
phone: (541) 574-3100

Project Access
www.projectaccess.com

Disabled Sports USA
451 Hungerford Drive Suite 100
Rockville, MD 20850
phone: (301) 217-0960
fax: (301) 217-0968
www.dsusa.org

Jubilee Sailing Trust
Hazel Road
Woolston. Soton SO197GB
England
phone: 23 8044 9108
www.jst.org.uk

Disabled Sailors Association
64 Hambledon Road
Waterlooville, Hampshire
United Kingdom
phone: 1705 254254

HSA International

El Prado
San Clemente, CA 92672-4637
phone: (949) 498-4540
fax: (949) 498-6128
www.hsascuba.com

Moray Wheels
www.moraywheels.org

Live Dive Pacific, Inc.
74-5588 Pawai Place, Building F,
Kailua-Kona, HI 96740
phone: (800) 344-5662
phone: (808) 329-8182
fax: (808) 329-2628
www.livedivepacific.com

Dolphin Research Center
PO Box 522875
Marathon Shores, FL 33052
phone:(305) 289-0002 (program reservations)
phone: (305) 289-1121 (offices)
fax: (305) 743-7627

Budget Travel

Is It Really Possible?

Microtel
phone: (888) 771-7171
www.microtelinn.com

Motel 6
phone: (800) 466-8356
www.motel6.com

Travel Inn
phone: 1582-414341
www.travelinn.co.uk

Golden Access Passport
www.nps.gov/parks/passes_fees.htm

Chamber of Commerce.com
www.chamberofcommerce.com

Subscribe to *Emerging Horizons* today! Visit EmergingHorizons.com for more information.